EVERY FRIDAY
SHABBAT SHALOM
FROM A GENTILE FATHER
Blessings, Meditations, and E-Conversations

By Larry Rawlins
Cover Photos By Larry Rawlins

Copyright © 2016 Larry Rawlins

All rights reserved.

ISBN-10:1530984556

ISBN-13:978-1530984558

ACKNOWLEDGEMENTS

Thanks to the Rymans – Lamelle, Rob, Neshama, Aliya, Shalev (and Haya) – for being special correspondents and muses for my writing. I hope that this chronicle of blessed memory will have a special place in their individual libraries.

Thanks to my ever-young spouse, Melanie, for encouragement and helping me find time and house-space for putting everything together.

Thanks to Dawn Sweet for providing graphic editing and keeping our computers working.

Thanks to my former employer and the teachers' union for contracting a duty-free lunchtime during which most of these pieces were written.

Thanks to Abby for being an amazing toy poodle, and more recently to Ellie, our adopted *bichon frise*, who has become a super sister to Abby. They knew just when to interrupt to give me the breaks I needed to stay fresh on the job.

~ EVERY FRIDAY: SHABBAT SHALOM FROM A GENTILE FATHER ~

FOREWORD
By Lamelle Ryman

Dear Readers,

A treasured gift that came to me by way of my conversion to Judaism in 2001 was the support and acceptance I received – and still receive – from my parents. When people would ask how my parents had reacted, I loved to see the stunned looks on their faces when I replied, "Well, my Dad sends me a *Shabbat Shalom* email every Friday.

Once I first experimented with observance of the Jewish Sabbath (*Shabbat*), I was hooked. I love creating, in the words of Abraham Joshua Heschel, a weekly "palace in time," a day for connecting with loved ones, a day for study, prayer, food, reading, play, and rest. A day when we don't handle money and don't pursue a livelihood, reminding ourselves of the blessing of family love that sustains us. A day where all preparations for food must be completed in advance so that one is freed from menu planning and cooking for a cycle of daily meals, starting with Friday night dinner. A day when electricity is used only as set up in advance (with lights and hotplates on timers), and cellphones and computers are left alone. A day when we walk to wherever it is we want or need to go, appreciating and experiencing the seasons and the details of the pathways that are lost in the blur of a car window.

Over the years, my parents have adapted to our "going dark" for 25 hours each week (plus certain holidays for which we embrace the same restrictions on using electronics) As we have observed Shabbat in their home and ours, I think they have intuited what is true for me: As the world of technology and communication spins faster and faster, Shabbat is a stabilizing and centering force for the Ryman family.

Receiving the weekly *Shabbat Shalom* emails from my Dad in the beginning years of marriage became a touchstone. Rob and I would print the email but wait until candles had been lit before reading it. The emails were thus interwoven into our ritual and rhythms as a couple while experiencing the highs of an incredible year exploring Israel, adopting our first rescue dog, the bliss of newly weddedness, cherished new friendships and community in Los Angeles, pregnancy, moving across the country to NYC, and the ineffable transition from couple to family with the birth of our first miracle, and lows of losing friends who were killed by suicide bombers during the second intifada in Israel, 9/11, the loss of our first pregnancy, and then a harrowing prenatal diagnosis. You won't read much about those events here, except in passing – but it is important to know that they were lurking in the background. With each passing week, no matter what was going on, the poems and blessings and stories poured out of my Dad and washed us, steadily, with love.

Now, more than a decade since his retirement from active duty as a school counselor I am filled with gratitude as I imagine him sitting at a gray metal desk in a room with giant ceilings and cheerfully decorated walls, taking time from his busy day to write and to connect. It has been ironic (and frankly, alarming, since he is a creative genius with much to share) that in retirement, he seems to have had less time to write. But this book represents a new season. Like the dry bones in Ezekiel that will one day live again, he breathed life into these word-ly blessings and resurrected them, cementing their importance both for future generations of family lore and for their broader appeal to friends and family who care (and perhaps to those who don't yet know that they care). It is our deep hope that this book will be the first of many to come – books encompassing both his collected past writings, and writings yet to be.

Dad and Grandpa, we love you and we thank you.

Lamelle, Robbie, Neshama, Aliya and Shalev
(with your adoring grandpets, Sofie and Buki . . . and the spirits of Haya and Chupey)
May 1, 2016
23 Nisan 5776

CONTENTS

	Preface	i
1	2001 C.E. ~ 5761	1
2	2002 C.E. ~ 5762	5
3	2003 C.E. ~ 5763	45
4	2004 C.E. ~ 5764	81
5	2005 C.E. ~ 5765	119
6	2006 C.E. ~ 5766	135
	Afterword	147

PREFACE

As former United Methodists, our daughter's chosen spiritual path in Judaism elicited for us a kaleidoscope of feelings, frustrations, and learning opportunities. We might have anticipated her conversion of heart and soul, because we purposely parented our only child with her developing free will in mind. Nevertheless, lines from the old waltz, "Daddy's Little Girl" – "You're the Christmas angel, my star on the tree; You're the Easter Bunny for Mommy and me . . .." – have a more-than-ever sense of melancholy when they come to mind. Although Jewish traditions are legendary, Christian folk, too, have fancied up more than a few over a couple of millennia.

While inevitable, it is also counterproductive in a family to be concerned with comparisons – shul and church, Epiphany and Rosh Hashanah, Chanukah and Christmas, Easter and Passover, Sukkot and – hmm . . . church camp? So what's a father to do? I chose acceptance and support. I accept our daughter's chosen spiritual path and support her as she articulates or demonstrates need.

Some of the challenges encountered with our daughter's conversion dealt with kosher food shopping, religious holidays, and "Shabbat (Sabbath)" - no automobile travel or electronic communication from sundown Friday to sundown Saturday. Anticipating Shabbat prompted an opportunity for a series of e-mailed messages from me to our daughter and her family, mainly conveying the blessing, "Shabbat Shalom." The following is a four-year-or-so chronicle of sorts of [usually] weekly communications for and with our daughter, her significant others, and ultimately for whomever might find them amusing, comforting, challenging, or just readable.

~ EVERY FRIDAY: SHABBAT SHALOM FROM A GENTILE FATHER ~

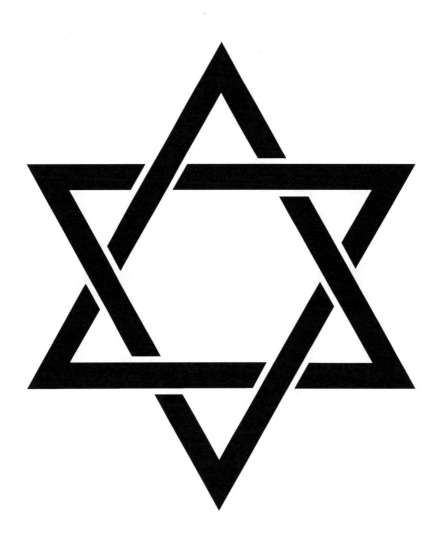

~ EVERY FRIDAY: SHABBAT SHALOM FROM A GENTILE FATHER ~

~ EVERY FRIDAY: SHABBAT SHALOM FROM A GENTILE FATHER ~

2001 ✡ *5761*

~ EVERY FRIDAY: SHABBAT SHALOM FROM A GENTILE FATHER ~

~ 2001 EARLY PRACTICE ~

The first emails were about anticipating the kids' return from their yearlong Dorot Fellowship in Jerusalem, and their getting settled in Los Angeles, California.

To: Lamelle & Rob
From: Larry Rawlins
Date: June 6, 2001
Subject: **Erev Tov**

Just one week from today –
May this week and the intervening Shabbat be full of peace and promise.
May your final moments *this* year in Israel fill you with the wonder of what you learned and accomplished.
May your tears of loss cleanse your eyes so you can see what soon you will *begin* to learn and accomplish.
May your heart feel the love that comes your way with this message.
May you love each other and life as long as there is breath that speaks your names.
May love guide your steps and words wherever you go.
I love you.
Dad

To: Lamelle & Rob
From: Larry Rawlins
Date: June 8, 2001
Subject: **Shabbat Shalom**

Love can't:
Be pushed around in a wheelbarrow
Zoom through space on a rocket
Be thrown into a basket
Be hauled into court
Leap into a lap
Be executed (unless, perhaps, in the execution of a contract)
Be driven
Be physically restrained
Be blown away by the wind
Be devalued on Wall Street

~ EVERY FRIDAY: SHABBAT SHALOM FROM A GENTILE FATHER ~

> Love can:
> Be the energy that pushes the wheelbarrow to share life's heavy load
> Move faster than rockets between two receptive hearts
> Be kept in and recalled from baskets and other cherished mementos
> Flourish without judgment
> Create a sense of being in the lap of luxury no matter how low the bank account
> Be created within a freely accepting mind
> Drive our behavior
> Provide beautiful boundaries within which there is ultimate freedom
> Seem to be "blowin' in the wind"
> Earn more interest than the wealth of nations
> Be yours, ours, always
> Love, Dad

To: Lamelle & Rob
From: Larry Rawlins
Date: June 11, 2001
Subject: **Erev Tov**

Dearest Adult Children,
Still tovly bokering around here. Day after tomorrow we'll, all of us, test organizational skills, crisis management skills, reality, temporal deference, stress management, adaptability, pro-social skills, sleep deprivation effects, transportation endurance, T-cell responses, adrenaline intoxication, and anxiety – especially test anxiety. So, look out for each other, be kind, sleep as much as you can in transit, and consider the enormous positive impact you make on America when you are here. Consider also that the rest of us, here, will reduce our collective anoxia, because we will breathe easier when you will have returned.

You probably noticed the subtle (in case it really was subtle this might unsubtleize it) use of the future perfect tense in the previous sentence – Our future will be more nearly perfect and less tense with you nearer – 5 time zones closer is so cool!
Love through all time and space,
Dad
P.S. Los Angeles highs are in the high 60s to low 70s this week, in contrast to our 70s and 90s.

To: Lamelle & Rob From: Larry Rawlins Date: December 16, 2001 Subject: **Shabbat Shalom**
As the fire of eternity disappears once more May your hearts be full of light and warmth. As you light candles of remembrance and hope May you feel the presence of those who love you. As darkness tries to overcome May your own radiance erase every shadow. Happy Hanukkah! Much love, Dad

~ EVERY FRIDAY: SHABBAT SHALOM FROM A GENTILE FATHER ~

2002  *5762*

~2002~

To: Lamelle & Rob Ryman
From: Larry Rawlins
Date: January 11, 2002
Subject: **Shabbat Shview**

Hi,

I ran across an essay contest on the internet, so dashed off the attached. The contest is sponsored by Andersen windows, of which we have many in our house. The theme is how the "view" from our house has "inspired" us. I haven't actually, or even unactually, submitted the piece, but thought you might enjoy it.

Rob, we send you shared concern regarding Nettie, and hope that you enjoy your time with her during this weekend, as you are fully present for her. Please convey our best wishes to her and to Sandy and Sy. Henry and Andrew too, are on our minds and in our hearts. Be proud of your beautiful, talented family of origin.

Love and peace to both of you on Shabbat and always. Remember to use time wisely before time uses you.

Love, Dad

To: Lamelle & Rob Ryman
From: Larry Rawlins
Date: January 18, 2002
Subject: **Shabbat Shalom**

Dear Kids,

May the energy
To overcome life's inertias be
On your tongue like sweet wine,
In your vision like candle glow,
In your lungs like fresh air,
In your hands like fine-tuned instruments,
In your muscles like the dance,
On your mind like family,
In your ears like beautiful music,
In your heart like love,
And may you move
To the rhythm of destiny.

Love, Dad

~ EVERY FRIDAY: SHABBAT SHALOM FROM A GENTILE FATHER ~

So it began: Those (usually) weekly meanderings of meter and connection across the boundaries of nations, states and backgrounds via the electronic superhighway. Most of the remainder of the work will not be shown in the pseudo-email format used above.

January 25, 2002

Something About Stars

I don't know why or how this thought began – something about stars –
I only know that every beginning had something to do with stars,
And now, here I am trying to discover why stars are important.
Star-struck?
No, just struck by the beauty of their pivoting patterns.
I've never seen one that had facets like diamonds,
Or five or six discernable points,
Or an Oscar.
Yet this fascination with stars seems to bring me closer
To millennia of stargazers, star worshipers, and star travelers –
Facts and fictions about how to keep from being lost,
How to explore the unknown from trans-Atlantia to Io,
And beyond our spare galaxy –
Han Solo to Leif Erikson to 21st Century Astronauts –
Where to look for Bulls and Bears
Excepting the stock market and Chicago athletics.
If we were to be star-like,
We would shine somewhere
All of the time, insofar as we understood time,
And we would guide someone lost
To some safe shore,
And we would be a source of wonder
For all of our twinkling
And we would inspire composers to write music
And children to sing,
And we would occasionally join
In binary systems
And dance through nothingness and eternity
Amazing and thrilling star voyeurs,
And we would model steadfastness,
Because as long as a generation might live,
They would see us always there
Where we always were
Where we always dance
With flair and passion
And always with each other.
Aren't stars something to be about?
Love, Dad

There was no time for dwelling on, editing, or reworking anything. These were to be spontaneous, in the manner of Ira Progoff (a psychologist who promoted Intensive Journal Writing): "Put pen to paper [fingers to keyboard] and write," which I learned in workshops with Dr. Sidney B. Simon.

February 1, 2002

The Light

The mighty Mississippi flows through bows,
As fingers twinkle on the way to stars,
And intellect takes up the fight and spars
With darkness ever gone because it glows.
And ravens come and, with them, darkling crows,
To fly afar the path of space to Mars
And clear the way of evidence of scars
And free the stem from thorns, the blood red rose,
To feel the freedom now and ever more –
Result of living with some lofty goal –
We go unyielding straight into the night
And know that knowledge lies beyond some door.
Across a threshold flies our very soul
Toward the knowing part and point of light.

February 8, 2002

Birth Memory

What was the sound –
That first unfolding sound of life?
What was that grand cacophony
Of earth and flesh and light and taste,
Of discomfort, cold and gravity?
What was the noise
That made the first impact –
The silence after?
What let us know about belonging?
When did we begin to sing
Inside our brains in imitation of
Future melodies,
Always remembering the *first* sound,
Always listening to the *first* memory,
And knowing, somehow, that there is more –
What was the sound –
The sound that sings love?
Love, Dad

I have a sound-based birth memory that I would recognize if it could be heard again. But that is unlikely, isn't it? LDR

~ EVERY FRIDAY: SHABBAT SHALOM FROM A GENTILE FATHER ~

February 15, 2002

'Possum Story
Once upon a story time,
And twice upon an opening mind,
There lived a 'possum family tailfully swinging from the tip-top branch of a tree,
The self same persimmon tree that had served that family for generations of stories.

The 'possum – or were they plurally 'possa? – families,
Past and present, cherished their tall, fruitful tree,
And did what they could to keep it strong and healthy.
They were careful to keep from clawing or gnawing the bark too much;
They were sure to eat fruit only when it was ripe;
And they left some fruit to fall
To start new trees for new generations of 'possums – or would that be 'possumim?
Some young 'possums – 'possumi? – were feeling crowded.

It seemed that all of the 'possums – 'possumos? – of past generations were living in the tree
And all of those elders bossed them around too much –
"Don't go so fast. . . don't go so slow. . . don't eat that . . . practice playing 'possum."
And so it would go, night after night,
Because, since they were _____ [nocturnal] animals,
They only griped between twilight and dawn.
The elders were making some younglings anxious.
Two younglings went looking for a new persimmon tree.
Finding persimmon trees in the forest was not difficult,
But finding one that seemed both safe and spacious was not easy.
"This one is so low a fox could leap up and get us," they agreed.
"This one is too tall. To fall from such a height would be disastrous!"
"This one is even more crowded than our family's tree," said one.
"Yes, and those 'possums – *sic;* they were American 'possums, after all –
Didn't look like the kind I'm wanting to live around," said the other.
They were about to give up, when they heard a rustling of leaves nearby.
They looked at each other, then whispered in anxious chorus, "Fox!"
"What shall we do?" Whispered one.
"Can't run, can't fight, guess we'd better play 'possum," replied the other.
No sooner had they plopped onto their sides
Than the biggest, reddest, pointiest-nosed, fox in the forest arrived.
It prodded them with its hot, dry nose.
It pawed them with its sharp-clawed feet.
It took tentative nibbles of one hairless tail.
Then, seemingly accepting that these were not prey worthy of pursuit
By the most noble fox in the forest,
It proceeded to . . . *lie down right next to them and go to sleep!*
'Possum 1 and 'Possum 2 were perplexed, as you can imagine.

Never, in all the generations of possum lore,
Was this ever said to have happened.
Contributing to the problem was the uncomfortable fact that
'Possum 2 was in dire need of relieving a long-neglected bladder.
Changing positions was out of the question.
So there they all lay – 'Possum 1, 'Possum 2, and Slumber-Fox.
Communicating with each other was impossible.
"If only we had gone out looking for berries with everyone else," thought P-1.
"If only we had been content with our own tree," thought P-2 – who was fighting off P-3.

After what seemed hours – because it was –
Mega-Fox stirred, stretched, and rose to all fours.
Curiously, it poked P-1 and sniffed and pawed P-2,
Before deciding to stride away.
The 'possums waited longer than they thought they needed to,
Then P-2 got up and did a natural forest thing
Before both of them lumbered stiffly back to their beautiful persimmon tree.
They arrived just as the eastern sky was glowing fox-red
And shuddered as they climbed to the safety of their branch.
Mom and Pop 'possum were just swinging into their places.

"We missed having you with us," said Mom.
"Yeah," said Pop. "We had the greatest feast ever. Where were you two?"
"Uh, we were around," said P-1, suddenly very hungry.
"Yeah, we were checking out some new territory," said P-2.
"Well, you missed a great night. Great food, great fun.
"And you should have seen everybody fall over all at once,
"When Uncle Reynard came in dressed like a fox and drunker than a skunk."
The younglings gulped together.
"Yeah, that must have been a riot," chuckled Possum 1,
With a sick feeling in an empty stomach.
"Yeah, I'm sure we're both going to stay with the group tomorrow," said Possum 2."
Then, with a collective yawn, and thankful to be together,
The whole family went fast asleep,
Just as the sun began to burn like a candle's flame atop the eastern horizon.

Love, Dad
P.S. Possum stories were a sometime-bedtime event for Lamelle.

~ EVERY FRIDAY: SHABBAT SHALOM FROM A GENTILE FATHER ~

To: Larry Rawlins
From: Lamelle & Rob Ryman
Date: Sunday, February 17, 2002
Subject: **Re: Possum Story**
Dear Abba,
The Possum story was wonderful…thank you so, so, so much!!!!
I love you.
Robbie and I look forward to passing on these stories to the next generation of possums someday!
Love love love
Ldr

February 22, 2002

In the Beginning There Was Music
And the Conductor raised a baton
And the universe rushed to orchestra seats,
And hushed, expectant for the symphony of ages

And the baton came down, an ictus,
And the percussion of the first movement
Snapped and boomed and rolled and rang
Across the ethereal audience, who were moved to new relationships,
Transported to new consistencies,
Established in new configurations,
By the power of the music.

Another sweep of the baton, an ictus,
And the first taut string vibrated,
Followed by others, and others, all possible sizes,
A full spectrum of amplitudes and frequencies
Sweeping from one space corner to the other
Becoming first melodies, first harmonies,
Tempering all in their wakes with beauty.

Another ictus,
And some bellowing brass-wind sound,
Like a trumpet section of star-sized elephants,
`From some deep depression of space,
Sped in all directions establishing presence.

Again the ictus bounced,
And the purest wave wove sound
Calling forth living organisms,
Which echoed all they heard.

The baton evoked again,
And throaty, woody, reediness was borne
Through time on gentle waves of need,
Balancing and complementing what was.

The repeating swish of the baton
Brought a sense of pulse and predictability,
And rhythm and regularity
Made first attempts at domestication.
And then the tip of the baton
Made a little circle in space
And all became quiet,
Allowing rest for weary harmonics
And time for universal constructs
To savor the new reality.
And this new perspective
Seemed excellent,
So the rhythm of rest and silence
Extended to the continuing composition.

Because of this primordial music,
Lives have shape, stress, release, and hope.
When we listen with our souls,
We hear the Beginning.

Love, Dad

~ EVERY FRIDAY: SHABBAT SHALOM FROM A GENTILE FATHER ~

March 1, 2002

Presence
Listening for the sound of presence,
The voice of companionship
The song of friendship,
The sigh of loving,
Hearing the percussion of footfall,
The rustle of cloth on cloth,
The hum of contentment,
The melody of conversation,
The whisper of close;
Believing there is something greater,
Which as we move, communicates –
Wordless, meaningful moments of music –
The harmony of belonging,
The counterpoint of freedom.
May you ever listen for each other
As we have always listened
And known presence.
Love today and all days,
Dad

March 8, 2002

The Puffy Fluffy Playful Puppy
The soapy, slippery, sudsy puppy, shampoo in her hair
Is getting a bath, which she's happy to share.
The wet and wildly playful puppy, runs here and darts there,
And dares us to catch her but avoids every snare.

The feisty, squirmy, wriggly puppy, doesn't like to be brushed;
She hopes that her human will hurry, will rush.
The puffy, fluffy, playful puppy is proud of her curls,
And prances and dances and jumps and twirls.

The puffy, fluffy, playful puppy, her hair dressed in bows,
Sniffs the sharp winter air with her cold little nose.
The puffy, fluffy, playful puppy on a dusting of snow,
Leaves paw prints behind her wherever she goes.

The puffy, fluffy, playful puppy is in a hungry mood.
She sniffs at her dishes and waits for her food.
The puffy, fluffy, playful puppy curls up on your lap.
She's played through the day and now needs a nap.

Shabbat Shalom, Dad

March 15, 2002

Today

Today we remember yesterday
And plan for tomorrow,
But most of all
We just live the day out,
And we take what we get
And make the most of it.
Some todays can be difficult
To get through,
But there is usually some kind of balance
To the aggregate of days
That keeps us going forward
Without stagnating
Or recommitting errors.
Be aware of your responsibility to each day –
To learn from it,
To take the best of it
And build a positive and robust future.

Love, Dad

P.S. Today is niece Delores's birthday – took her 4 months to catch up to me.

~ EVERY FRIDAY: SHABBAT SHALOM FROM A GENTILE FATHER ~

March 22, 2002

I was just reading about myself.
At first I thought I was reading about a student.
But the more I read, the more I realized
That I was the subject and object of each sentence.
This worn tapestry of life seems to
Spread itself across generations.

Because there are those who
Pummel, pull, push, and crumple
Our fragile fabric,
We see ourselves darkly in others
And say, "There, but for the grace of God, go I,"
Never really getting it –
"There, but for the grace of God and the subjective justice of genetics, go I."
Now scientists can read the whole human genome.
That's sort of like taking every book that was ever written
And saying that it's merely a collection of alphabet soup.
There you go – Jack Canfield's next best seller –
Alphabet Chicken Soup for the Human Genome.
So we go – selling ourselves
On the auction block of corporate slavery
And consumer-based economics
And regression toward the mean.

How is it possible that this generation
Must struggle with the same nonsenses
Of generations past?
There must be no real, positive, elevating evolution
When it comes to *the* human struggle.
Divine intervention is required for any society,
Where to "be all *you* can be"
You must join the Army.

So I read about myself,
Never meaning to – just sort of happened –
And I learned something more of me,
Not really wanting to know,
And maybe a little late to put it to good use in my life.
Maybe, though, I can help that kid,
Whom I thought was the object of my reading.
Maybe by helping this child *in* time
I'll help myself *through* time.
Maybe something is evolving, after all.
Maybe . . . .

I'm still not sure this is finished, and I'm not sure I want it to be.
Love, Dad

March 27, 2002

Hi Kids,
Just a note to wish you a Happy Passover with blessings, including, but not limited to, good health, good company, good nourishment, good memories, good plans, good respite, good history, good future, good hugs, good house hunting, good fortune, good savings, good luck, good herbs, good bread, good wine, good miracles, good mitzvot, good goods, l'chaim in 5763 and always.

> *Home is the sailor,*
> *Home from the sea,*
> *And the hunter home from the hill;*
> And the counselors home from the convention.

Good to hear a bit of Lamelle's lilting voice yesterday. We were home at about 8:20 – 10 minutes shy of 5 hours (two stops). The convention was quite good, but the "helpful" on-site publications were less useful than other years. We managed. I listened again to *Ashira's* Joint CD on the way to work this morning. I think you ought to do a studio CD.

Enjoy each other; have a perfectly wonderful Passover together. May the plagues of human destruction and malevolence pass over us and our extended, unknown, and collective family throughout the planet, and may we know peace and true freedom in our lifetimes and bring honor to those who left us the legacy of caring for the world and each other.
Love, Dad

March 29, 2002

Whenever I Think of You
Whenever I think of you my soul smiles
And I feel something eternal continuing
As from some previous eternity.
This is no epiphany of faith or transcendental flight,
It's just a moment
When bliss is a mental image, still glowing,
A recalled conversation, still pursued,
A treasured touch, still warm,
A shared wine, still sweet,
A realization of newness, still young.

Thinking of you now and ever in love,
Dad

~ EVERY FRIDAY: SHABBAT SHALOM FROM A GENTILE FATHER ~

April 5, 2002

Certainty = Death and Taxes

Old saw cutting into consciousness -
But what about other certainties?
Like survival instincts?
Like fight or flight?
Like procreation?
Like hand, and food, to mouth?
Like learning and adapting?
And what about their extensions?
Like cooperation?
Like healthful living?
Like loving and honoring?
Like feeding each other?
Like knowing and teaching?
And what about their extensions?
Like achieving goals?
Like balance?
Like caring and nurturing?
Like feeding others?
Like being and appreciating?
And what about their extensions?
Like identity?
Like fairness?
Like healing?
Like equity?
Like being appreciated?

What must happen for living and giving to be certain in the world?

Shabbat Shalom, Dad

To: Larry Rawlins
From: Rob & Lamelle
Date: April 8, 2002
Subject: **Re: Shabbat Shalom**

Dear Abba,
I want to thank you once again for sending us your Shabbat Shalom blessings/poems/stories/musings…it is such a wonderful way to strengthen the connective tissue between us and I hope it continues for a long, long time. You cannot know its impact or fully appreciate its meaning for us. Thank you so much, again and again. I love you!!! Certainty = Love Unconditional, ldr

In 2000 C.E. Melanie and I visited Lamelle and Rob in Jerusalem, where they were Dorot Fellows. We hired a professional touring company to be our personal guides (and body guards), traveling in a Land Rover to experience Israel as most tourists might not have the opportunity. In 2002 there was considerable unrest in that area, I emailed the guide company to inquire as to everyone's safety and copied the ensuing conversation to the kids.

To: Lamelle & Rob From: Larry Rawlins Date: April 8, 2002 Subject: **Hello**
Dear Bernie, Fran, Amy, and Gilad, Just wanted all of you to know that we are thinking of you at this time and hoping that you are all well and safe. We have treasured memories of ca. 16 months ago, when we were guests, with Lamelle and Rob, in Jerusalem; and when you helped us have an unforgettably beautiful experience from the Golan to the Dead Sea, the Dig, the Flour Caves, the Kibbutz, the museum/bunker overlooking the Brown Line into Syria, etc., etc. We hope that this historic struggle in your neighborhood will be over, peaceable, soon. I can't imagine that you have been able to function in your business even at the limited level of December 2000. Wishing you the best life can offer, Shalom, Larry (and Melanie) Rawlins

To: Larry Rawlins From: Heidi Stern Date: April 9, 2002 Subject: **RE: Hello**
Dear Mr. and Mrs. Rawlins: Thank you for your note. Bernie and Fran are on their way to China, and are well. I left your message for Gilad, and spoke to Amy who is well, and appreciates your concerns and sends her regards. Be well, Heidi S.

I received the following from Rob.

To: Larry Rawlins From: Lamelle & Rob Ryman Date: April 9, 2002 Subject: **RE: Hello**
Dear Abba Larry: This was a very, very sweet thing that you did. Love, Robbie

April 12, 2002

Futures Market

Who would like a free future?
I've one to give away,
But don't expect immediate delivery.
I have more past to leave behind
Before letting go of tomorrow.
Once I'm done with today
Tomorrow will be yours to give away.
That's the real essence of parenting –
The gift of single futures
That compound into cultures
And create beauty and build dreams.
When my future becomes yours
I trust that you'll build your own
As an honorable estate
To be passed on to honorable heirs.
It is unthinkable to take possession
Of a future and use it to ravage the world
With wars, wickedness, and selfishness,

Yet many, unthinking, in history and in our time
Have done horrible deeds,
Which tear apart the fiber of humanity
And take away the futures of so many.
Invest, instead, in futures of strength –
Those institutions that care for the weak
And restore their rightful robust natures;
Those that treat others fairly
And nurture everyone to fulfillment;
Those that leave the world better
For our precious heirs.

Love and blessings,
Dad

April 19, 2002

Reflections on a Rainy Day
Remember the lines from some other times
About drought and the thirsty earth?
Well it's diff'rent times now for these dry lines,
Because of water there is no dearth.
Two inches plus, by now maybe three
Of rain has blessed garden and tree,
And raindrops that once
Would be soaked up as bunce
Are cast off to the rivers and sea.
On roads to and from work,
In low spots it lurks;
The streams are all rushing and straining,
As vapors once airborne, now body regaining,
Fall, filling all blank space remaining.
We welcome the greening of garden and grounds,
And even like hearing the thunder,
And we know that as long as it stays well in bounds,
The water will not put us under.
What metaphor, then, or now as it were,
Should I pluck from the storm-laden air?
Perhaps it's enough to let our hearts stir,
When water falls here and/or there.
Or the meaning of life perchance only floats
When buoyed by the love in our being,
And viperous words demanding our votes
Fill not the future we're seeing.
Or enough is enough of anything good;
It's better to wish its returning,
Than to wish it a toothpick instead of a wood,
Or a match when the forest is burning.
Love, Dad

~ EVERY FRIDAY: SHABBAT SHALOM FROM A GENTILE FATHER ~

April 26, 2002

Spring is really here!
The boat is bound to the dock.
Forsythia and magnolias are blooming.
Red buds are burgeoning,
Branches hang heavy and green with potential.
It is April; there are showers;
And no snow is in the forecast.
Winter's puppy marvels at all things, new,
Especially earthworms, surface-bound by rain.
Clean deck furniture is placed alongside colorful plants,
Potted with care and hope.
Air is sweet and swift.
Night skies alternate between jeweled spectacle
And low, quick clouds reflecting Earthlight.
Maybe some day I'll live away from seasons' displays.
But this one day I'm happy at home,
Knowing that spring is really here.
Love, Dad

May 3, 2002

What would we know of dreams –
Conscious representations of the unconscious mind;
Symbolized, encrypted thought,
Visual, auditory, and kinesthetic memory in Technicolor,
Parts of mind, unfinished business?
To dream, asleep or awake, is to select from one's mental fabric
Threads of self, thus emerging from the loom of life,
Bringing to mind those bits and bytes of experiences consciously unresolved.
These spikes of meta-awareness are best left in the Unconscious;
The U will prevail for You – in your best interests, when allowed.

One's vision of the future can only be a dream
When imagination is recorded as conscious thought.
One's dream of the future was decided at some past conscious level,
Clearly enough to be recorded for later access.
One's reality path begins with imaginations of want.

Assure *sogni dolce** with sweet threads.
Imagine sweetness in your life,
In all of the ways life represents sweetness,
Taste the honey; touch the texture; wrap in the fabric;
Keep the sweetness handy but unconsumed;
And live, consciously, each day, *la dolce vita***.
Love, Dad
*sweet dreams   **the sweet life

May 10, 2002

We do the best we can do –

As good as it gets –
One kid's best good
Is another's worst nightmare.
Ever wonder what we smelled like in grade school?
Probably a lot like the places we went home to each day.
I must have smelled like cigarette smoke,
Mixed with a little out-house and barn,
And wood smoke from the cook stove,
And eggs fried in bacon grease,
And yesterday,
Only slightly sweeter on Monday,
Following Sunday's bath.
Some kids smelled like cats, goats, or turkeys;
And Henry smelled so of wild garlic one day,
The teacher made him sit in the way-back of the room.
Fact is, we all smelled pretty much the same,
So who was to object to the olfactory assault?
Kids bathe more these days,
So it's harder to sniff out their home environments.
It would be easier to write social developmental studies
If we could smell the kitty litter,
And dog dander,
And shared bedrooms,
And smoke,
And fried catfish,
And booze and ooze.
Fact is, thanks to soap and water,
We all smell pretty much the same.
But my era was more honest,
Because a kid like me had a better chance
Of being accepted as ordinary.
Kids are still being raised by folks
Who are doing the best they can.
If that's as good as it's going to get
I may just wrap up in an old nightmare
And try to sleep through it.
It's late. Are you still awake?

Shabbat Shalom, Dad

The preceding followed a home visit I made on Tuesday. It wasn't pretty, so the piece isn't either. At least that family has a house to be in and sleep in. I love you. Enjoy each other. Pats to Haya.

May 17, 2002

New
As fresh
As never before
As young
As unspoiled
As curious
As searching
As inexperienced
As healthy
As novel
As original
As primitive
As primary
As rudimentary
As elementary
As budding
As every moment of every day
New
Enjoy the newness today and every today.
Love, Abba R.

To: Rob & Lamelle Ryman From: Larry Rawlins Date: Friday, May 24, 2002 Subject: **Shabbat Shbirthday**
1. Love 2. Peace 3. Knowledge 4. Groundedness 5. Hope 6. Vision 7. Experience 8. Ability 9. Decisions 10. Understanding 11. Truth 12. Justice 13. A better American way 14. Solutions 15. Empathy 16. Assertiveness 17. Joy 18. Spirit 19. Togetherness 20. Awe 21. Caring 22. Cooperation 23. Meditation 24. Satisfaction 25. Future May these 25+ words for the years of your life, Lamelle, be a source of thoughtful contemplation. Happy birthday. You have been the source of my most thoughtful contemplatings for this quarter-century. You're next, Robbie. Both of you please enjoy being momentary age-mates.

~ EVERY FRIDAY: SHABBAT SHALOM FROM A GENTILE FATHER ~

May 31, 2002

Something Zanier Today
We're off to see the wizard,
The wonderful wizard of Zane.
We're having a spate of a blizzard,
Of snowiness melted to rain.
So harness your lizard
And bless your sweet gizzard*,
It's folly to be over-sane.
Our friends and we are dancing
The two-step and rock and roll waltz.
The polka is very entrancing
And the cha-cha has very few faults.
So muzzle your lizard
And bless your sweet gizzard,
And keep all your money in vaults.
The night is quickly approaching.
The sun is 'most over the hill.
The shadows are darkly encroaching,
And the waiter has brought us the bill.
So nuzzle your lizard
And bless your sweet gizzard,
And keep your hand out of the till.
The times, they are a wonder –
The goofiness, sadness the same.
We'll follow the King of the Blunder,
And ride the wild beast 'til it's tame.
So saddle your lizard,
And bless your sweet gizzard,
And gallop on to the next game.
The verse may be way too silly
And frivolous, zany to boot,
To be published in N.Y. or Philly,
But who gives a holler or hoot?
Just get off your lizard,
And bless your sweet gizzard,
And wait for the signal to shoot.

Bless your sweet gizzards and their human analogs. Shabbat Shalom, Dad

*"Bless your sweet gizzard" was a Jacquetta Golden phrase, which was used as others might say, "Bless your heart." The gizzard was one of her favorite parts of the chicken at mealtime – a piece I never coveted.

To: Lamelle & Rob Ryman From: Larry Rawlins Date: June 7, 2002 Subject: **On the importance of living in a multi-faceted universe where a full moon signifies beginnings of marriages and werewolves and where natural den dwelling puppies must be protected from den dwelling coyotes and where fighting in school gets students suspended and fighting on T.V. makes millions for book makers and where that doesn't have anything to do with books for enjoyment or learning and where most things we do are gambles and where we continue to continue because of intermittent reinforcement and where we seek the importance of life whether we feel important or not and where our importance is of little consequence to most people and where we are important to one other soul, living is important**
Joy through love makes living worthwhile. Shabbat Shalom, Dad

June 14, 2002

Shabbat Shapuppy

Abby has been helping me with the yard today.
She supervises better than many school administrators.
Best of all, when I get close to where she is tethered,
She seems truly glad to be near me.

Did you notice that the letters in Abby can also spell "baby?"

She's in that post-toddler stage now –
Yearning for independence; into everything; so brave,
Until an unexpected sound or visitor sends her into a lap or a frenzy.

Our friends have arrived to share the weekend.
We anticipate much laughter and a good time in the sun and water.
The puppy will have one more new experience,
And we will talk about the new times for our babies.

Enjoy each other and Haya.
Attend to the latter and learn.
Breathe freshness into your love,
And talk about new times.
Love, Dad

~ EVERY FRIDAY: SHABBAT SHALOM FROM A GENTILE FATHER ~

July 12, 2002

We won't be home today or tomorrow,
Traveling to take care of other business.
We anticipate with delight
A near future opportunity to stay home
And water flowers, not in a rush,
And pull weeds from a verdant garden,
And go, not so far away, to play golf –
That blissful, sometimes frustrating walk in the park –
And we will enjoy stars from the "crow's nest,"
And wilderness from the water,
But most of all we will enjoy being together at home.
May your weekend find you at home, too,
And may you feel our weary, but glad, presence
In your hearts each minute renewing life with you.
Love, Dad

July 26, 2002

Shabbatot Shalom
People must have been molded from dust.
We react the same way to natural nurturing.
The dust around here hadn't felt rain for weeks –
Though this present dust was less dry than some.
Last night we got about half an inch of rain.
And, you know what? None of it went anywhere,
Except down, where it fell.
No lakes formed in flat fields, and
No great gushes of runoff
Raced through our westward swale.
The water fell where it was needed,
And the need soaked it up, sponge like,
To be squeezed through thirsty roots
To make grain for some other need.
Let us wish for a world where there is no drought,
Depriving soil or human spirit.
It has been said that "rain falls on the just and the unjust alike,"
Yet we humans have more control over whom we dispossess of what,
So let us prove that human justice can fall on everyone,
No matter if they are wet or dry,
Or green or purple, or young or old,
Or quick or slow, or rich or poor;
Let us live justice for humanity
One drop at a time;
And let it be soaked up
By a grateful, healthier world.
Love, Dad (Sorry for missing last week)

August 2, 2002

Wirdsmytheen
Inglish iz foney the weigh wirds are raught.
Wyth sew many waze four coundz to get caught
Inn alfabett soop, en taip, and on dysk,
Wee halve tu bee breiv, wea muhct teik uh rysc,
And speech it oar rye tit two bea understood,
Too cumyunikate fieleens and faktc az wee shood.
Soah dohnt geht dyskureijd, or made, or uhpceht.
Wen wurds are spehled dyfrent than cowndz that wee ghet,
Inglish iz foney, sough guhced laf it ough;
Wenehvr ewe wunder: coff, cauph, or cough?
Luhv, Dade

August 9, 2002

If things go the way they ought:
Soldiers' time will be spent more in training, less in fighting.
Spring will water Summer's growth for Autumn's harvest.
Winter will provide beauty, recreation, rest, and sojourns warm.
Teachers will teach, students will learn, administrators will help, and bureaucracy will out.
Lakes will be made to conserve water and provide wholesome recreation.
Prodigals will return repentant and reformed.
Health will return to the infirm.
Families separated will be reunited.
Melodies - the whistleable kind - will return to music.
Harmony will be an apt metaphor for societies.
Faith will be neither blind nor blinding.
The cards of life will be played in the order dealt, and
The last hand held will be full of trumps.

Love, Dad

~ EVERY FRIDAY: SHABBAT SHALOM FROM A GENTILE FATHER ~

August 16, 2002

Wooly Worm Philosophy
One warm, wild
Woolly worm
In winter
Woke and wondered
Where to wiggle,
When a wisp of wind wound
'round and whispered,
"What do you want, and why?"
"Well," whistled the woolly worm,
"What I want is a world
of wonder,
a world
of welcome
wanderings
without war,
where water
is for quenching
thirst, not squelching
neighbors,
a world without
widowing, which
makes me wail,
a world where walls
are for windows
and fun family photos,
a world with
warmth in winter,
wealth enough,
and wisdom enough
to weave a wake
of goodness
whenever we walk,
wherever we walk,
roll, crawl, float, or fly,
a world of
winners
willing to help
the weak and meek
make their way
in the world, too,
and a world in which
men and women
won't squash
woolly worms
just because they can."
Love, Dad

August 23, 2002

No Time Like the Present

Please tell me that it will never be too late to laugh,
Never too late to feel the exhilaration of a moment,
Make amends for misdeeds,
Forgive,
Walk, hold hands, or enjoy intimate company,
Marvel at the sight and scent of a rose,
Accept love from a child,
Play,
Give tummy scratches to a trusting canine,
Do good work,
Listen,
Change,
Set a good example,
Explore more of the world, and
Revisit favorite places;
But *if you* were to tell me that
It will never be too late,
That would be a lie, and I won't ask that of you.
One day, it will be too late, and
That is why I am laughing *now*.

Love, laughter, and blessings,
Dad

August 29, 2002
Tomorrow

Dear Kids,
We are having a family reunion at our house tomorrow. Be advised that your attendance is mandatory, womandatory, and caninedatory, respectatory. There will be K* and U* stuff in the kitchen, along with fresh (!) garden tomatoes, peppers, zucchini, egg plant, and cucumbers (with a few straggling leaves of lettuce). There will be music, laughter, hugs, wedding wine, and anniversary cake. There will be heartfelt joy and a refreshed spirit from being together. Love will be the centerpiece of the table and the house will glow without the aid of fossil fuels. Furthermore, parents will not feel like fossils, nor will the children apprise them of any similarities.
Gotta go.
Love, Dad

*Kosher symbols on food products

August 30, 2002

Just Wondering

When did wonder go out of style?
There were times when it was easy
To wonder what one would find
At the end of a rainbow,
Or over the next hill, and
Why:
Is milk white, when cows eat green grass?
Does water run, when it has no legs?
Do the little birdies disappear from Mommy's fingers
(*Two little birdies sitting on a hill:*
One named Jack and the other named Jill.
Fly away Jack . . . Fly away Jill.)
Only to reappear in the next instances
(*Come back Jack . . . Come back Jill.*)?
Does the wind blow?
Do stars twinkle?
Do plants grow so big, then shrink and die?
Does summer sizzle, autumn fall, winter freeze, and spring thaw?
Does music sound like music?
Do we have different languages?
Are boys and girls different?

Wonder was easier at an age of improvised reason:
Milk is white because cows chew away the green in their cuds.
Water runs on tiny legs called bubbles.
The birdies just visit Heaven for a moment, but they're not ready to stay.
The wind blows because the earth is hurrying around the sun.
Stars twinkle because they're trying to talk to us.
Everything grows up, then their seeds make more of them, and then they grow down.
Seasons change so we won't be bored.
Music is music because our ears know the difference between plain and pretty.
We have different languages so we won't get bored with the same old words.
Boys and girls are different so they won't get bored.
Boredom is a state of mind that says the grass is greener elsewhere;
But there's always some old cow chewing her cud there, too.
Love, Dad

September 6, 2002
Roshing Along (Rosh Hashana 5763)

One would expect the head of a year to have a brain. Why not?
Year brains are probably little different from human brains – or bird brains for that matter. What does matter is that the brain has been recording a lot of stuff over the past year, and a lot of what has been recorded, if not outright junk, is caked in the mud of washed out ideas, awash in dripping idolatry, and strung out on the webs of unkempt sensuality. What makes human (and bird) brains a little different is the ability to go inside our brains and do virtual house cleaning. Birds do this more easily than humans. They have automatic cleaning systems that start them fresh every day. Humans hang onto the old stuff far too long.

So enjoy the house cleaning. What an awesome thing, to travel through your brain, just riding your mind to wherever it takes you, sponging up the greasy residue of poor decisions and indecision, attacking the enemy of free thought, right-ism, and opening up the closed parts, especially those parts that block the wisdom of others or see only in the dimness of shuttered vision. And as long as you're there, you might as well clean out the olfactories – you might find yourself sneezing, if necessary – and just get rid of the freeway smog, the highway skunk road kill, and the gourmet delight that became alight and smoky and undelightful – gone forever, except as a chuckle on remembering.

And remember those unused, unopened boxes in the attic – things you "had" to put there, but which have not been useful since? Either toss them into the dumpster and be done with them, or give them to someone else who needs them.
And, since you may be going to the dumpster, anyway, you might as well take out those feelings of dread, failure, and disappointment that are no longer useful in any way. Remember to save and cherish the useful stuff.

When you're done with the cleaning, be sure to care for your cleaning tools before you put them away. Undoubtedly, you'll need them again – probably before another year passes; and you want them to be in good shape and immediately available, don't you? Now, look around inside your brain, clean up any crumbs of anger or dysphoria. Be sure that all channels are tuned in to the most useful input. Give it one more rinse of living water, and then step back and realize what an awesome thing you have done, and you can say to the world, "I'm ready for another year."

Love and Shannah Tovah, Dad

| To: Larry Rawlins |
| From: Lamelle & Rob Ryman |
| Date: September 6, 2002 |
| Subject: **Re: Roshing** |
| Dear Abba, |
| Wow. What a beautiful and powerful metaphor (I cheated and read it before tonight! Couldn't wait!). It will be a wonderful meditation for us to ponder as we inaugurate the New Year. I'll hopefully give you and mom a call this afternoon. THANK YOU SO MUCH! Funny that you mentioned living waters (mayim chayim), since I was just at the mikveh last night. Ldr |

~ EVERY FRIDAY: SHABBAT SHALOM FROM A GENTILE FATHER ~

September 11, 2002

In Memory of a Year Ago
On Hearing Copland's "Quiet City" on WIUM on September 11, 2002

Who will play the trumpet when all is past?
When there is no future, who will play the last?
What floor holds the dance that lately I am learning?
What chances are there, then, of all that was, returning?
By what authority is presence here assigned?
Have we earned this place with our own kind?
Or have we but taken, and taken for granted,
As princes and presidents raved and ranted?
Will there be a future fomenting new life?
Will there be such a thing as husband and wife?
Will our world collide with one unknown?
Will we reap exactly, precisely what's sown?
Will there be a time when we can't look ahead?
Will there be a moment when every word's said?
Or will grandchildren, hence, find new sea and strand?
Will the new destiny be one, which we've planned?

Love, Dad

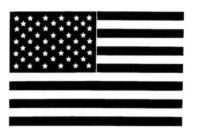

September 13, 2002

Shabbat ShRules

Is the rule of law necessarily the rule of reason?
Is reason always the best perspective? Consider Spock.
To rule justly one must associate with the ruling and the ruled.
To rule according to a rubric one suspends personality.
What arrogance to believe oneself just!
May the explicit and implicit rules in your lives,
As well as the hidden contracts between you and others,
Serve you kindly and justly.
Choose your rules carefully,
Enjoy the comforting anchor that rules provide,
And flourish in that soil.
And remember what rules are made to be.
Broken rules may become tomorrow's rules.

As is my rule, I leave you these hurried thoughts, and rush on to other matters –
none so precious as the matter of love, which is my rule.

Love, Dad

September 20, 2002

Shifting Gears
Nature shifts gears when it's least expected.
Wet and windy, then Wham!
Drought and grasshoppers.
Farmers from my era knew the most about nature's gear shifting.
It was a farmer named Murphy who discovered:
If rain is needed have the hay cut and in windrows.
If rain isn't needed have the hay cut and in windrows.
If the equipment breaks down this morning, it will rain for two weeks, straight.
If the equipment has just been overhauled, the weather is great, and the crop is ready,
the fuel truck will break down and the tank will be empty.
Under the previous circumstances, when the fuel finally is delivered,
A storm will soon follow.
This is why farmers became such great philosophers.
It's also why so many of them were poor.
But the poor make the richest philosophy:
Hold on 'til tomorrow, and everything will be O.K.
Maybe next week/next month/next year (sounds a little like Cub fans) . . .
It's not so bad to be poor when everyone else is, too.
If you can't do one job well, take on two or three – at least, you'll have an excuse.
Never admit that you like or want subsidies.
Never borrow money unless you can borrow money to pay it back.
All money is borrowed and one day must be returned with interest.
The main thing is this:
No matter what calamity careens into your path,
Be prepared to shift gears and travel a different road.
It may take some time to get up to speed,
But after a while the old road will be nostalgia fodder.
How many calves can you raise in Manhattan on that diet?
Love, Dad
P.S. There may be some ruralisms that aren't readily apparent to the generationally removed. Your turn to ask questions.

September 27, 2002

Blessings of Farm Life
"The blessing" was what we said over each meal before we were allowed to eat a bite. To a child such a delay can be torturous. Our real blessing was that we recited the "Family Prayer," mercifully brief – "Dear Heavenly Father, we thank you for this food. Bless it and bless us. Help us and guide us. Amen." – easily done in a single breath. So the HF blessed the food and us, I suppose, and nobody died of botulism – proof that faith and prayer work.

We were blessed also to have high quality meals of sufficient quantity to sustain our bodies and support our physical labor and mental faculties. Farm fare in those days consisted of fresh vegetables – lettuce, cabbage, tomatoes, onions, sweet corn, peas, green beans, beets, peas, and potatoes; three sources of meat – beef, pork, and poultry; peaches, apples and pears; eggs; and milk – enough to drink, make into cottage cheese, sell, and feed to the hogs. When we had a calf butchered we had the steaks cut thin, so they could be fried in a skillet. The potatoes were sometimes fried in the meat grease with onion slices. More often, the potatoes were mashed. Naturally, the leftover mashed potatoes were made into patties and fried for the next meal (not too unlike latkes).

Another blessing was for the family to be able to sit at the same table for meals. It was *Mom's Law* that breakfast was at 7:15, dinner was at 12:00, and supper was at 6:00. This varied only at harvest time or when some fieldwork needed to be finished before a rain. The variation was played out as field delivery at the appointed hour.

We were blessed with fresh air; meaningful work that had a beginning, middle, and end; helpful neighbors who were, in turn, grateful for our help; and a variety of animals to pique curiosity and responsibility.

So enjoy the blessings of your unique life. You will look back some day with shaking heads of wonder.

Shabbat Shalom, Dad

October 4, 2002

Shabbat Shlonely
(Mom is gone and I'm playing bachelor for a couple of days.)

It's a dark morning in Illinois. That autumn is here holding back the sunrise would be enough, but today's sky also holds dark clouds that are neither translucent nor reflective. Thanks for your call last night – a bright spot in a less than stellar evening. I did get the hands-free phone fixed. Abby had chewed through the cord while Mom was using it some time ago. Had to let it charge up overnight to test it, and it works. Those wires are really miniscule. That's why I used solder to mend them – not enough stuff to work with for the usual twist and tape splice.

It's been a long time since I did serious electronic soldering – since way before you two were around. In 1968 I was stationed at Fort Leavenworth, Kansas, in the 371st Army Band with a guy named Litchfield, who was a stereophile with an engineer's mind. He had designed and constructed his own speaker cabinets and put his own stereo system together, so a few of us got the specifications from him and commenced work on our own.

There was a stereo retail store in Shawnee Mission, Kansas (about a 45-minute drive), which had bought at police auction a truckload of Wahrfdale speakers. A thief had filed off the speakers' serial numbers, so they couldn't be marketed as new products. The store was selling these high quality, 12-inch, 3-way speakers for $25.00 each – an enormous bargain, but, along with other necessary components, a serious financial commitment for us.

Herschel agreed to have a student in his high school woods shop class make the speaker cabinets out of solid walnut for which we would pay. I supplied him with the Litchfield specifications, and as the cabinets were under construction in Maryville, I started work on a Cortina 3700 amplifier kit in the basement of our rented one-bedroom duplex in Leavenworth. This was my first experience with electrical soldering. Before printed circuitry every transistor, capacitor, resister, etc., had to be soldered into place with acid-core solder. It was the same roll of solder and the same soldering iron that I used last night to fix the phone. Both performed well after 34 years of disuse.

In January 1969 my Cortina kit was about 90% completed when I got orders for Vietnam. Since I wasn't sure that I could get the amplifier finished before I had to leave, the store manager in Shawnee Mission reluctantly, but magnanimously, agreed to trade my in-progress amplifier kit for a factory-wired amplifier for the difference between their regular new prices – about $30.00 as I recall. I was determined to (1) hear our own stereo before I had to leave [in case I was in no shape to hear when I got back] and (2) share the sound with Betty and Herschel (an attempt at inspiration for them to get something nice for themselves).

We went to Graham that weekend psyched to install the speakers in the walnut cabinets and listen to the new Phase-4 recording of Ted Heath's orchestra. The cabinets were absolutely beautiful, *and they were about two inches too narrow* – Herschel had not noticed that the student mismeasured.

Not-too-daunted, Herschel and I went to his high school shop on that Saturday. He selected some veneered plywood from the school stock and proceeded, with a little help from me, to cut, glue, stain and finish new cabinets. After drying overnight, we picked them up on Sunday and assembled the aggregate stereo components in the Nelson's piano room. Pushing the power switches, putting needle to groove on the Dual 1240 turntable, and the world of state-of-the-art stereophonic sound filled the house.

Following Vietnam, Melanie brought the amplifier and turntable with her when she joined me in Hawaii. I had purchased 2-way Coral bookshelf speakers and a TEAC 1500-A reel-to-reel tape deck in Vietnam, so we managed with that setup until we established a home in Tecumseh, Nebraska, in the fall of 1970.

Our stereo systems have changed many times since those days – maybe no more or less than we have changed   yet we still use our "original" speakers, and they still sound great. I wonder what the next generation of sound reproduction will be and if these speakers will have a part in it. Have a sound weekend full of music of the heart.
Love, Dad

October 11, 2002

Shabbat Shlate

Mom bit the dust; she fell asleep at the computer, so I shall carry on. We went to a "Rockapella" concert tonight followed by a reception at the University President's home. Rockapella was terrific. I had a good conversation with the bass singer at the reception. I started to listen to the first Harry Potter book on tape today. I really like it. The writing style is somehow familiar, but I can't place the antecedent. Better get to bed (it's midnight); I have two meetings in Canton tomorrow, but I probably better go through Avon on the way (which it isn't). Time for Progoff:

Measure of Love

If I were to measure love,
I'd have it stand up in the doorway
With its head up high as it would go
And I'd mark a spot on the doorframe
For all to see
And for all to wonder
At all the marks going from
Down there
To here
To up there
As it grows and grows,
Not quite like a child,
Who, when reaching a certain height,
Tends to stabilize, then diminish;
No, the love marks keep going
Up and up and up
Till you can't exactly see them
Up so high,
But you know they're there
Ever higher
Ever growing,
Because that is what love does.

Love always; goodnight,
Dad

P.S. Remembering that this is my mother's birthday – her 99th.

October 18, 2002

Not About the Sunrise
There was a perfectly museful sunrise this morning,
But I'm not sure that words could ever do it justice,
So this piece is not about the eastern sky
Over western Illinois on October 18, 2002,
Because of the inadequacies of dictionaries.
Awe is a precious state.
People have become too narcissistic
To revere much outside themselves.
When possessing awe-ness one would
Rush along the northward road
And slowly ply the eastward path,
Prolonging the headfirst plunge into light and color.
If something as grand as this morning's sky
Can evolve from beautiful to more beautiful
With each glance over half an hour,
And all the while not working at it,
Rather merely being what it is,
Isn't it reasonable that, with spare effort,
Each of us is capable of continuous,
Progressive, enlightened metamorphosis
In the course of a whole, brief lifetime?
Love, Dad

October 24, 2002

Dear two and Haya,
I'm going to be on the road tomorrow, so I'm not sure Ill be next to a computer soon enough to write, hence *Shabbat Shathursday*.

Now and Then
There are times when being in the present is all that is necessary. To know the *Now* and to focus on our center can be a reassuring, relaxing state. I think that I do that some, but I also like to live through time as well as in it. To live through time, I am conscious of all the yesterdays and planning for all of the tomorrows. *Now* is just that transient click of time between the two that can't be sustained. To focus fully and exclusively on *Now*, though useful at times, is to deceive oneself into believing that *Now* is sustainable. It isn't. However, one use of *Now* is to forgive and prepare our selves for *Then*, on each respective side of *Now*. Enjoy each *Now* of Shabbat. Create joy for each other and celebrate the newness of each moment together. Sparkle or glow as your light allows, and hear the symphony of love in each other's voice.
Love, Dad

November 1, 2002

Fall In

Abby had her birthday yesterday.
There was cake, one candle, and singing.
There was a gift, which she opened with a little help.
Then she carried it away, sure it was a toy
(Everything is a toy, even the birthday poodle).
Probably she was disappointed to discover that it was clothes.
She does look cute in it.
Poodle time marches on.
November – just these two remaining months of '02.
Trees have been lately colorful,
But their beauty remains bittersweet, mourning
The accelerating, looming loss of vestments,
Though in a way leaves become toys and art
For the earth-bound after gravity's triumph.
And horizons become lower
And sunsets slower
Without leaf shadow in westerly eyes.
It must be the metaphor of autumn.
Love, Dad

November 8, 2002 (my 58th birthday)

Shabbat Shyoung

Dear Kids,
One day I will be old.
This is not the day,
For today I have things to do,
Places to go,
People to help.
Feeling useful today,
How can I feel old?
One day I will be unable
To drive a car,
Play racquetball,
Dig in the garden,
Water ski.
This is not that day.
Being capable and useful is youth.
The skin may lose a certain luster,
Certainly shape changes,
And the pate becomes pitiful,
But, given joy, youth is eternal.
Even in that distant future
When I find myself car-less,
Shovel-less, garden-less,
Racquet-less [heaven forbid ball-less], or ski-less,
Even then, with grateful and joyful heart,
I would be young as when
Jumping in hay stacks,
Riding bareback, jumping ditches,
Skinny-dipping in the pond,
Scratching chiggers,
Pitching in a real baseball game,
Digging tunnels through fence-high snow drifts,
Burning corn stalks across a field,
Playing a corn stalk fiddle, or
Listening for whippoorwills' permission to go barefoot.
So keep me around for a while longer.
One day, when I'm old,
I want to be totally used up –
Nothing left – *nada* – *niente* – *zilch*.
I must say goodbye *before* that happens,
But this is not *that* day, either.
Love, Shalom, and many a Mitzva,
Your young dad

November 15, 2002

Shabbat ShHands
Farm hands, ranch hands,
Helping hands, cool hand,
Lend a hand, handshake,
Green hand, handy,
Hands in the air, bare handed,
Hand tools, give a hand,
Left hand, right hand,
Wrong hand, other hand,
Hand me, hold hands,
Hand-me-down, hand up,
Hands up, hands to yourself,
Red handed, Black Hand,
Handle, Handel,
Hand Hospital, hands down,
Callused hands, surgeon's hands,
Lost hand, ghost hand, off hand;
Give yourselves a hand
For being who you are,
With hands that are for holding, not hitting,
With hands holding onto the hearts of hope,
Helping to shape the next generation,
Grasping truth,
Letting go of pain and anguish,
Soothing and smoothing,
Lifting each other,
Pointing the way to peaceful tomorrows.
Hereto I affix my hand and seal,
Love, Dad

November 22, 2002
Shabbat Shsoon
Dear Kids,
I don't have much to say today. I'm happily anticipating being together. Each day I feel your presence wherever I am, and that sensation comforts me and brings smiles. The welcome prospect of sharing your space in a few days brings comfort and energy to a weary body.

Thinking of how easy it is to get on a plane and go wherever we would, and not to have to spend months crossing plains, rivers, mountains, and desert, as the early Euro-pioneers experienced the trek to L.A. environs, makes me marvel at the engineering feats of the past century, pausing to imagine a future full of similar changes.

Let the Rawlins-Ryman nations declare Love on each other and be fortified with unconditional positive regard. We are what we think before we are what we do.
Let's think peace and do what we can.
Love, Dad

November 29, 2002
Shabbat Shalom and Happy Hanukkah
Peace on Earth, and Blessed Be the Oil
Once you have heard the crescendo of the "blat, blat, blat," of the Chinook blades you will never forget it. The sound, blessing to some, curse to others, resonates with the present war. *The angry green giant flies toward us; stingers poised starboard and port; half hovering, half setting down; opening its anus in our faces, farting searing gales of jet exhaust; allowing entry into the screaming, deafening (vero!), guts of the beast.*

There are those who would have rejoiced to hear that sound, feel that blast, and could not, even when it arrived; some who feared its approach and ran; and too many who needed it when it was continents out of earshot and never forthcoming. Peace on earth should never mean R.I.P.

The success or failure of causes can depend on noise. As many people may be moved by "Green" issues as by NRA issues, yet the noise of one will nullify the reason of the other. So let's resolve to make "joyful noises" in the New Year. Let's trim our wicks with care, so the lamps will burn with great economy. Maybe that's the way to bring joy to the world and peace on earth. And, above all, let's begin a crescendo of joy that will stifle the cacophony of fear around us.

"Blat, blat, blat" – What a useless noise for those who are beyond rescue! What a fearsome warning to those who do others harm! What a joyous sound for those who await rescue or transport! There's a time and place for everything; let's make some noise and light some flames for justice and peace in our time and place. Blat!!!
Love, Dad

December 6, 2002

Just Last Week

I remember anticipation,
Like knowing that at some soon moment
The sun would divest itself of earth's modesty
And leap stark naked into morning.
I remember calling and knowing you were near,
Like vibes, like anxious comfort, like before.
I remember the trunk lid popping,
Like some rare, prescient, carnivorous plant demanding, "Feed me!"
I remember the calm, warm air,
Like the love-blanket Everymom spreads over Everychild.
I remember the first hugs and kisses,
Like honor, like unconditional acceptance, like *only* the first.
I remember being there before,
Like familiarity, like affirmation of the firmament, like hearth and home.
I remember playing,
Like puppies who spar life-lessons,
Like inner children allowed outside for fun.
I remember concern,
Like nurturing spirit sprinting across time zones.
I remember the mountain's top,
Like a stone cork in a green-brown bottle,
And I remember touching the bottom of the top,
Like an achievement to enjoy again.
I remember surf-sound from Highway 1,
Like a siren's rhythmic whisper, "Yesssssssssssss."
I remember nourishment,
Like food, like soothing touch, like spiritual vitamins.
I remember clean-break-leaving at the airport,
Like feeling fuller but lighter, like marking the point of return,
Like knowing.
I remember these things and more,
Like the wish for you to have joy together,
Like today, tomorrow, and always.
Shabbat Shalom, Happy Hanukkah,
Dad

December 13, 2002

Shabbat Shabusy
It's been a busy day in Lake Woebegotten. I covered MS Chorus – we watched a little bit of West Side Story and talked some about gangs. I have repaired a couple of band instruments. And I worked on our mailing list on and off, between other regular stuff. About ready to go home now, so will do a quick piece.

Do the following for each other:

Sit down. Breathe. On purpose.
Harvest oxygen. Feed carbon dioxide to the plants.
Ever notice how just focusing on your breath helps you to relax?
Of course, I would never tell you to relax, because that could imply that you are anxious.
So, whatever you do, don't relax. Just pay attention to your breathing.
Notice its regularity or irregularity, the sound of the air moving in and out, in and out.
Be aware of the way the chest, shoulders, and abdomen respond to each breath.
Try holding your breath, then resume breathing before that becomes uncomfortable.
Notice what that was like as you continue to breathe normally.
Imagine that you are breathing in a color and breathing out another color.
Realize that each breath draws in healing and expels dis-ease.
What color heals you? What color are you getting rid of?
Paint peace with healing color.
Feel gravity. Notice how much stronger it is now than a few moments ago.
Give in to gravity. It's reassuring to know you won't float away into space.
See points of light and choose one as yours.
You already know how to welcome light to your being and how to accept its healing.
How much better will you feel in 2.2 minutes?
Light, color, and breath: Enjoy playing with them as you begin to feel better and better
With each breath.
Love Dad

December 20, 2002

Welcome Home

The Rymans and Hymans sailed off in a plane
To Can Tho and Bangkok– Just why? Can't explain.
The Hymans and Rymans away from it all –
The hustling and bustling and tunes – "Deck the Hall!"
What fun! To go somewhere with nary a care
And find in the strangeness traits that we share
With cultures so different and customs diverse,
To learn: tolerance, acceptance, and love's not a curse.
And learning these things all about all these others
Will help all be better World's sisters and brothers.
So, while you're in Asia, the part called Southeast,
Have fun, *exotica*, and feast after feast.
And visit the high points and some of the lows,
And hurry home safely; fly straight as the crows.
And tuck in your memories the gems of this time;
Remember that Ryman and Hyman still rhyme.
So Hymans two, Rymans, too: Glad that you're home!
We look forward to pictures and stuff from your roam.
And Happy New Year, in two thousand and three,
And every year after we know as C.E.

Love, Me

2003 ✡ *5763*

~2003~

To: Lamelle & Rob Ryman
From: Larry Rawlins
Date: January 10, 2003
Subject: **Shabbat Shahome**

Dear Ones,
I have a complaint.
I am complaining that people complain too much.
So much belly-aching about this or that government policy,
Or this or that bad meal at a restaurant,
Or the price of gasoline,
Or public schools,
Or taxes,
Or tax relief . . . .
O woe are we, going to hell in a poorly designed basket
(Made by the lowest bidder for a government grant)
That we can't afford.
Such whining!
Hats off to those who actually write to their elected officials.
Kudos to those who accept their own and others' efforts as excellent –
The best they can do given the resources and circumstances –
Rather than expecting perfectly impossible perfection.
Felicitations to those who expect no more from others than from themselves.
Congratulations to teachers and administrators who do everything they can
To become better and better,
Regardless of how often their chains are yanked
In pointless, one hundred eighty-degree directions.
Thanks to the conscientious custodians of the "common good,"
Who use our community wealth for the enrichment of all.
And praise to the Constitutional Convention,
Which devised a plan that makes it possible to change
Leadership, personnel, and style,
By a mere mark on a ballot.
There should be a shot-clock on complaining,
Such that, if no action is taken by the time the clock runs out,
The complainer would be shipped off to the "Third World" for perspective.
Keep working. Keep on doing. Shine.

Love, Dad

January 17, 2003

Shabbat Shworld

Who wants a better world?
Raise your hands up high.
Who wants to be the one
To cast a better die?
To Live in Peace with little care
Is something to be treasured,
To give a piece of self somewhere
Is one way we are measured.
Who wants a better world?
Who robs us of its promise?
In pain we weep for assurance gone,
And hope someone can calm us.
Each one of us can do some part;
Each day we live we share our heart
With those whose days are early past.
And in our living well and long
Mock the moon-maligned at last
And make a world that is steadfast,
That sings a different, better song –
"I want a better world today,
In peace I want to live.
I want a better world always;
Who has that world to give?"
Remember with each crumb of bread,
Each glass filled o'er the brim,
That better lies inside each head.
So be a better world today
Than that we knew before.
Who you are and what you do
Will shape it to its core.
Love, Dad

January 24, 2003

Shabbat Shtgif

Dear Kids,
Just a little nightcap,
The end of a week of work,
A TGIF *a la* UU at our place –
Few people attend –
Cold, sickness, conflicting events –
Nonetheless, fun had by all
And food to nourish the body
And entertain the palate.
Shabbat shalom, children of destiny.
Take the peace that is beyond understanding
And live and thrive in it.
Take the love that comes with this message,
And be buoyed by its uplifting presence.
Take the knowledge of knowledge
And lead a world to peace.
Be cool, stay warm, and improvise.
Love, Dad

January 31, 2003

Shabbat Shlucky

Dear Kids,
Maybe fall and spring are best. A brief opening turn of the window crank and the sun and green and blue and gold of the out of doors become extensions of our living space. The fickle surface of Spring Lake ripples, reflects, surges at the bidding of the breezes. At a time when we must consider conflict in our nation, this is a welcome, enveloping place of peace.

The grown family arrives too seldom; yet enough to join us with wonder and awe at world-class sunsets reflected in the water. To have this refuge where once-children want to return is reward enough for the keeping of and caring for it. The mown lawn or shoveled driveway, as the seasons dictate, invokes their presence and approval. We watch the endless road in anxious anticipation of each blessed visit.

In winter, the flickering firelight might be enough to remind us of the meaning of "hearth and home." Add to the blaze graceful, glistening airborne vessels sailing past a backdrop of pine and naked oak, anchoring in our garden harbor, and one knows the beauty and comfort of being home, of being warm, and of being very, very lucky.
Love, Dad

February 7, 2003

Shabbat Shaloooooooooooom!

Dear Kids,
We used to sing
"The answer, my friend, is blowin' in the wind . . . . "
There is no new melody,
And there is no new lyric
To cause us to reflect.
"How many seas must a white dove sail
Before she sleeps in the sand?"
The old melody lingers in the ether
And beckons ears to be open to the tune.
We used to sing
"Where have all the flowers gone?"
There is no new melody.
And there is no new lyric
To cause us to reflect.
"Gone to grave yards every one.
"When will they ever learn?"
When will we ever learn
That the echo of the old melody
Resounds in counterpoint
To the percussion of the new order.
When will we ever learn
That blood should stay inside our bodies?
That breath begun deserves a chance
To respire for decades hence?
That love transcends tribulation?

Have a blessed weekend, full of Love.
Love, Dad

February 14, 2003

Shabbat Shavalentine
Love

In the mysteries of time,
In the evolution of evolution,
The most profound construct is the least tangible,
Wearing many faces,
Walking as many paths.
Still we know it
And still we find it,
Though we may be neither going there
Nor looking for it.
As evolving Family we cherish this gift
Above all others
And give this gift
As is our free choice,
Accepting our place in the mystery.
Love, Dad

February 21, 2003

Shabbat Shpeace

Dear Kids (and Grand Dog),
May you feel peace in your house and hearts,
May you see love in every gaze,
May you seek wisdom from flowers,
May your fortune be enough,
May your plans be full of promise,
May your memories bring smiles,
May your passions evoke actions,
May your voice sing and speak truth,
May your rest heal and resurrect,
May you wake happy for the day's opportunities,
May you always know the comfort of companionship,
May you accept inward and outward change as necessary,
May you recall the voices and warmth of those who love you.
Love, Dad

February 25, 2003

Hi Kids,
Below is my most recent email to Kent and Ginny, including the little song that grew out of our visit. Hope you like it. Hope you are doing well. We're fine, although our Sable, with Mom at the wheel, was hit by another car on Friday. Mom was in the left lane on East Jackson, near K-Mart in Macomb, when another car, apparently following the car ahead of it too closely swerved left to miss that car and hit ours instead. His left side got our right bumper and door. Both vehicles remained drivable and nobody was hurt. I think the other driver got a ticket.
Love, Dad

Together Heart to Heart
Drinkin' decaf. Coffee
Eatin' key lime pie.
Playin' double-twelve dominoes;
See the sunset sky.
You and we are family;
It's not a calamity
That we live so far apart.
When we get together,
No matter what the weather,
We're together heart to heart.

Shoppin' in the afternoon
After lunch at Chili's,
Bundle up against the chill.
We'll be home by half past nine,
Out of beer and no more wine,
Feeling like we've had our fill
Of fun and games with lots of style,
Enough to last a little while,
Again we'll get together soon.
Though we live so far apart,
When we get together,
We're *together heart to heart*.
[Repeat 1st stanza]

February 28, 2003

Slow Children Playing
When, as a child just learning to read,
I noticed signs of the road.
Some, like STOP, were clearly useful.
Others, though, made me wonder:
YIELD was a word I had no use for.
NO PASSING seemed redundant on midwestern hills.
The one that gave me greatest pause
Is one still seen some places:
The sign declares,
"SLOW CHILDREN PLAYING,"
And I felt so sorry for the kids and their folks,
Because why should the passing world need to know
That the children in the nearby house are slow?
Isn't it amazing how misunderstandings
Materialize for want of a tiny comma?
And if something that small can make a big difference,
Can't we choose to make a difference toward a better world?
Better for children, the slow and the quick,
Better for parents, the thin and the thick,
Better for life's punctuation.
Stay safe and healthy.
Love, Dad

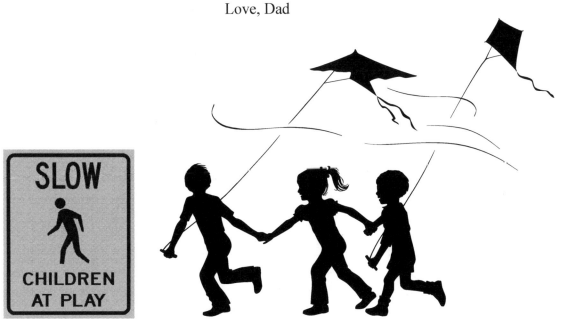

The following two pieces are responses to an email essay from Lamelle declaring that we are all "tiny dots . . . creating little ripples around us. . . ." I suspect it was an unneeded defense of her decision to discontinue her studies at UCLA Law.

~ EVERY FRIDAY: SHABBAT SHALOM FROM A GENTILE FATHER ~

March 7, 2003
Re: Morning Musings

Dearest Dotter,
Thank you for your morning musings. Your dots remind me of an epiphany of sorts for me – I think you've heard the story of when I was in the fourth grade at Amity. Maybe I was involved in a game or just luxuriating on a warm spring day, lying in the cool grass during recess. I remember watching a blade of grass being blown about by the wind, and musing, "Even a single blade of grass makes a difference in the atmosphere. Because of that blade of grass the powerful wind has been parted and can't continue the way it started."

People displace much more air and interrupt its flow to a much greater degree than a blade of grass. It's not that we're important; it's just that we *are*. I wondered about trees, buildings, cities, and mountains, and the atmospheric influences they must have, concluding the obvious by comparisons to a blade of grass and me.

As I look back on the event, I am aware that at that time Layton was a senior in high school, Esther and Jack, Kent and Betty, and Mom and Dad were all farm folk. Irma and Frank were the mavericks; they were teachers in California. I was pretty sure that I would "be a farmer like my Dad" and other family members. And that would have been O.K., except that I just never felt like what I imagined a farmer would feel like. I had nothing against dirt and physical labor; there was just something that told me, "this is *not* who or what you are." So I had an opportunity that none of my siblings had or exercised (Layton dropped out of M.U. after one year and Kent went to Tarkio College for just a year). I went to college and majored in the one thing that I knew I was good at, because no one since Mrs. Bartlett (7th and 8th grades) had ever suggested that I had other talents (she saw me as an English major). I was a good music major. Then I met your mother, and little else mattered. I was never the greatest-ever music teacher or band director, but usually I was confident in those roles.

Choosing one's life path has a great deal to do with the feelings of identity one has with a proposed role. You couldn't readily identify with lawyering, so you wisely took a furlough. One's life path has little to do with choosing fame or fortune, except that one relishes the notion of becoming famous or wealthy; rather those who do well at life often end up becoming role models for others. It follows that fame is defined as being a role model for multitudes. Those who do life well take care of themselves and others in such a way that wealth can accumulate, whether or not it was a sought-after goal.

To find pleasure in good company with a song in one's heart; to appreciate the tough lessons and enduring them for the sake of knowing; to understand and thrill that each blade of grass, each *dot*, is different and special as it relates to other grasses and dots; to feel the presence of unconditional love every moment; these things I pray for you. The influence of a blade of grass in the desert is different than the influence of one in a pasture or playground.

That's all for now. Many tufts of u-c love,
Dot Daddy

March 14, 2003
Shabbat Shadot

Dearest . . .
Once upon a time there were two dots.
.1 was constantly preening and posing before a mirror
As if on a stage or before a camera.
.2 often settled at the window watching the world go by
With nary a thought about appearance.
.1 was frequently interviewed by media dots
And pontificated ad nauseam about the economy
And other political and social issues.
.2 went to meetings of other dots
And they talked freely and frankly about the economy
And other political and social issues.
.1 played the stock market and the ponies.
.2 invested in mutual funds, saved regularly, and purchased some tax-free bonds.
.1 voted in every election, and the ballot was counted once.
.2 voted in every election, and the ballot was counted once.
.1 lived a full life.
.2 lived a full life.
The end . . . .

Be ever thankful
For the gifts of life and love,
For the opportunity to be role models,
For the understanding of place and promise;
And find treasures every day
From being together,
Luxuriating in caring caresses,
And living for Love.
Love, Dad

~ EVERY FRIDAY: SHABBAT SHALOM FROM A GENTILE FATHER ~

March 21, 2003

A Few Good Words,
Well placed, well intentioned –
That's what it takes to be understood
In a foreign country;
Or by your spouse, or children;
Or by your parents, or neighbors.

A few good words –
Kaptain Kangaroo words –
Like "please and thank you"
Will do wonders to smooth rough situations.

A few good words –
Presuppositional words –
Like "before you begin to 'X' you will 'Y'" –
May be all the therapy you need to get unstuck.

Just as there is no good bomb,
There is no good insult,
Or condescension, or sarcasm,
Or "constructive" criticism.
A few good words –
Courteous words –
Can save a friendship, a relationship,
Or the *Ship of State*.

A few good words over bread and wine
Can aid digestion, slow the pace,
Launch a religion, sanctify a place,
Make a friend, or smilify a face.

"I love you," is a phrase of a few good words.
When it's *also* "I, you love,"
The same words are even better.
Whether I/you is/are me/you or all of humanity,
If *everyone* meant these few good words
And said them frequently,
There would be no place for bombs or destructive dogma.

What are your favorite words to say and hear?
May they be in your ear;
May they be on your tongue
Each day of the year,
And keep you e'er young.
I love you,
Dad

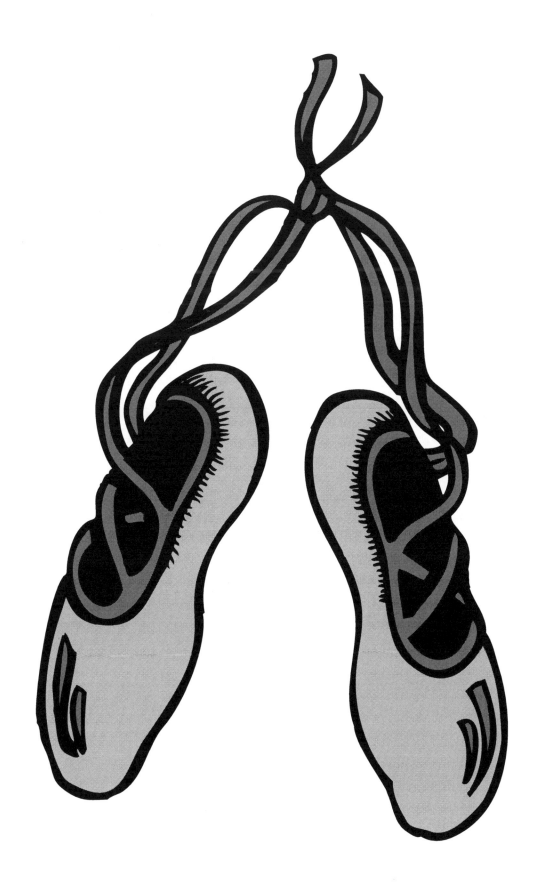

~ EVERY FRIDAY: SHABBAT SHALOM FROM A GENTILE FATHER ~

March 28, 2003

Paralysis and the Importance of Dance

Paralysis has many faces,
None of which move,
So that whatever is stricken
Is inert and dependent
On external forces for change.

Sometimes people are *paralysed* with activity:
They flit from one blossom to another,
Never taking enough time to notice
If the blossoms are natural or paper –
Rarely engaged in much that is real.

Other folk are *paralyzed* with perfection:
They complain of their own and others' inadequacies,
Never listening to their own words carefully enough
To realize that they are perfectly *paralyzed*
And that they will never be perfect.

Still others are *paralyzed* by idealism:
They want to do everything for everyone,
Leaving no stone or cheek unturned,
Seldom looking inward enough to know
The limits of what they have to offer.

There are some who are *paralyzed* by feelings:
They are so busy attending to themselves
That they are of little use to the rest of us,
Always focused on the first-person sensate,
Relating proportionate to others' promise of pleasure.

There are others who are *paralyzed* by accident:
They feel pushed, neglected, spoiled, or soiled
Into being unable to move,
Especially when the stakes are high –
Too high, in their minds, to reach from such a low place.

Some were *paralyzed* by choice:
It was easier, more comfortable, to remain at rest,
Watching the world move by beyond a window,
Than to interact with the world,
And thereby change it and themselves.

No one was ever *paralyzed* by dance:
Though at times most of us, in turn or collectively,
Feel too *paralyzed* to dance,
Those who move upon the dance floor
Are those most likely to climb the stair.

Let us hope for a world of dancers,
That we may be among them,
And that we experience *paralysis*
Only as brief, infrequent lessons, with important tests
That prove just how smoothly we can move.
Shalom, Dad

P.S. I'm not sure where this came from or might go. Dance is on my mind because we are going dancing at Sterling's birthday celebration tonight after pizza and wine with Bill and Jean at our place – possibly aboard the boat. I am reminded often of the following saying, which I have corrected politically, taught to us in the 7th and 8th grades at Amity by Katherine Bartlett:

Those who know not and know not that they know not are fools;
Avoid them.
Those who know not and know that they know not can learn;
Teach them.
Those who know and know not that they know are asleep;
Wake them.
Those who know and know that they know are wise;
Follow them.
Paraphrased from Confucius
Love, Dad

April 4, 2003

Shabbat Shapril
Dear Kids,
Blossoms, soft and fragrant,
Sunlight and shadow dappling,
Wind whooshing through willows;
April, warm and wet like kisses,
Welcoming the miracle of love
That you are.
Love, Dad

April 11, 2003

Dear Kids,
Just a few weeks since we were with you. And what terrific hosts you were! Thank you for sharing your home, your friends, your dogs, your music, your cars, your local and regional amenities – especially the Getty – and, most of all your love. We are so blessed!
I shall attempt a brief piece:

Elephant Jokes

Elephant jokes were way before your time, but you might have heard a few. I particularly like, "Why do elephants paint their toenails red?" and "How do you stop a charging elephant?" Others extant include, "What should you do to a blue elephant?" "What is the world's biggest ant?" and "What should you do if there is an elephant in your car?"

People are more like turtles than elephants; turtles are wannabe elephants that can't remember very well. Turtles see elephants standing around swinging their trunks, so they stick their own necks out just a little further. Turtles observe elephants wearing red toenail polish, so they develop intricate designs on their shells. People swing and strut their stuff very much like turtles. When they retire many people use portable houses – very turtle-esque.

As a bona fide, card-carrying Turtle, I approve of sticking one's neck out, being deliberate about where one is going, giving offspring maximum freedom to develop maximally on their own, ducking for cover when threatened, living near water, and knowing the right time and place to reproduce.

May your earthquakes be small, your heartaches few, and your headaches miniscule.
May your earth bloom, your heart beat love, and your head fill with wonder.

Shabbat Shalom, Dad

April 16, 2003

Let My People Go!
Spring is a good time for Passover.
Just as spring signifies renewal of growth
And emergence from the bonds of winter,
Passover signifies the renewal of the Jewish people as a nation,
Emerging from the bonds of slavery.
Whatever we may have become enslaved to
Over the past year,
Let us find freedom and renewal
In this spring's Passover
And emerge fresh and ready
To meet life's challenges.

Love, Dad

April 25, 2003

Shalom Shwhenever
Whenever a candle glows soft,
Whenever a tune stays in forethought,
Whenever glasses clink in salute,
Whenever doors open to new directions,
Whenever coin is the least precious part,
Whenever bread is passed,
Whenever voices speak of love,
Remember that we have shared those times, all together,
And rekindle the part of your hearts
That knows what family really is,
And trust that it will be always so.
Love, Dad

May 2, 2003

Shabbat Shacago
Dear Youngsters,
Mom will pick me up at school today and we will be off to Illinois Beach Resort in Zion, which is closer to Wisconsin than it is to the Chicago Loop. We will travel mostly familiar roads, so time is our only concern. This is for the Illinois Mental Health Counseling Association (IMHCA) Spring Workshop. I started those workshops – had the first one at College of DuPage – when I was President of IMHCA. Many of the people who attended that first workshop have been the leaders of the organization over the intervening 14 years. IMHCA picked up the ball that ICA dropped and became the driving force behind the successful establishment of counselor licensure in Illinois. I've only been to two other IMHCA workshops. They are supposed to keep some food warm for us if we get there late today.

Our yard has been beautifully arrayed of blossoms. The forsythia has dropped most of its yellow petals, looking mostly green, the red buds are waning, and the flowering crabs are just coming into their own. The hawthorn tree across the lane is in full white bride-bloom, and the apple trees are showing the promise of red deliciousness in a later season. We are, however, losing one of our large white pine trees east of the house – disease analysis in progress.

Our garden spots look vital, with bleeding hearts and iris already blooming and our lilac bushes perfumerous. Even the tiny, new flowering quince displayed orange color early, and the oak leaf hydrangea that the deer ate to the ground last year is sporting brand new green. Perhaps all of the roses made it through a relatively mild winter, and we replaced the white climbing rose on the west with a red one. The Easter lily in the house has one blossom left; I'll plant it outside this weekend.

Abby's sitter will look in on her while we're gone. The resort is pet-unfriendly. Mom, especially, enjoys Abby – not that I don't; it's just that Abby seems to be filling some void in Mom's life. Abby has her most photogenic poses, of course, when we aren't near a camera.

Have a tov Shabbat. Enjoy its calm and the internal peace that comes from having made important decisions. I hope your gardens are colorful and fragrant, that growth is happening where it's meant to be, and that love ever is blossoming.
Love, Dad

May 9, 2003

Shabbat ShMom

"There's no place like home. There's no place like home."
That and a couple of heel clicks might get you Kansas,
But home?
Home, being "where the heart is,"
Tugs at my heart all the time.
Heart?
Hearts get all split up – not necessarily broken – just split
As time goes on, and life is dealt hand after hand
Of winners and losers, royal flushes or pairs of deuces.
Hearts get split between childhood fear and adolescent invincibility,
From riding the training wheels out of sight, around the block,
To driving off to college, to diving into engagement,
To launching into marriage, to making life's decisions
About where and what home will be, and who will be there.
So it goes. . . .
"Hearth and home" is the familiar phrase.
"Heart and home" is more like life.
My mother was a believing "Dorothy."
For her there *was* "no place like home."
She knew where home was and who belonged there.
She was the "home *maker!*"
Home makers are, among other things, domestic administrators,
Judges, defense attorneys, prosecutors, cheer leaders,
Janitors, chefs, chauffeurs, and nurses.
Mom nurtured and helped prepare five souls to go from
Virtual training wheels, AKA scrapes and bruises,
To responsible tax payers, far flung across the country,
Secure in knowing that they could fling themselves "home" at any time,
And there would be bed for rest,
Breakfast, to order, whenever one awoke,
Dinner at noon, and Supper at six.
And when the home changed houses and states,
It was still home, because she *made* it,
And there is still no place like it.
Love, Dad

May 16, 2003

Shabbat Shmoon
We had a beautiful, natural spectacle last night – a full eclipse of the moon. Our best view was from the driveway in front of the house. I think we were the only ones of our neighborhood outside looking. Natural rhythms, natural phenomena are so comforting in a world where we are supposed to be in charge of ourselves and our environment. I am reminded of something my 7th and 8th grade teacher said: "If people along the jungles of South America and Africa were to stop cultivating crops and maintaining roads, the jungles would reclaim those areas for the wild within a year."

What kind of world would redevelop if we poor stewards were to be suddenly removed from Earth? I think that just a few decades hence, some celestial tourist might be impressed with Earth's unspoiled environment, clean water, balanced vegetation, and balanced animal food chain. It has taken a mere time-blip since creation (however one interprets that) for humanity to despoil the planet to its present vulnerable state. Nature has had much more experience with reclamation than humanity has had with decimation.

So, as we go about our controlling ways and days, certain that we are really masters of our fate, let's not lose sight of the possibility that Earth can get along just fine without us; we need Earth more than Earth needs us. So, as long as we're already here, let's take care of the air, the water, the ozone layer, the rain forests, and most of all, each other. If the ozone layer improves and none of us is here to enjoy the sunshine . . .

Find peace in your world, love in your hearts, and happiness always together.
Shabbat Shalom, Dad

May 23, 2003

Shabbat Shmove
Uncle Edgar said that his father killed my grandmother by moving too often. Think of post Civil War times – 1880s to 1890s. Probably the first move was from Iowa to Oklahoma – near Thurman to near Tahlequa.

Picture nearly 500 miles with horse-drawn wagons carrying all possessions.
Imagine a trip, which takes between 8 and 9 hours by car, averaging about 2 miles per hour – that's 16 miles in an 8-hour day and about 32 miles in a more likely 16-hour day – about 15 and half days' travel. And that's not counting crossing major rivers without bridges, following ruts for roads, enduring hot/stormy weather, gaining access to food, getting sick, being pregnant, caring for an infant – puts a twist on "Are we there yet?" doesn't it?
And the difficulties didn't stop at the destination. There was shelter to establish, water to witch, some kind of home to make, and two more babies – only Dad survived with the help of a Cherokee nursemaid, while his mother lay too ill to tend him, his older brother, buried nameless under red earth.

Then, as strength, and a rhythm of normalcy returned, the itch to move did, too. So the wagons were packed, and rut roads were located for the arduous trek across the Ozarks to the Missouri boot heel, only to pack again, with another newborn, Uncle Fred, for a return to Iowa, somehow by way of Arkansas and Nebraska. (The precise facts of the itinerary are buried with the older generation.)

Moving is one of the greatest stressors in life – and that's modern moving. Only a couple of generations ago modern moving would have looked like a delightful dream.

Delight in your dreams this night and always, and may blessings number as the stars that guided my grandparents across the American near west, which made this moment that is the two of you, together, possible.

Love, Dad

P.S. My grandfather was living his last year when I was born. I have no memory of him, except going with Mom and Dad to choose his headstone. Apparently he lived with a woman known in family lore as "The Old Lady" after Grandma died. All I know of my grandmother* is that she passed shortly after the return to Iowa. She was a diminutive, pretty (thankfully there is a photograph) woman, barely 5 feet tall, and by Uncle Edgar's accounting too frail for her husband's nomadic bent. Her maiden name was Merritt, and she was of immediate Welch descent, perhaps an immigrant.
*Josephine (Merritt) Rawlins

May 29, 2003

Almost
We're almost on our way.
A couple of hours left at work
Before the trek north to MLI
It'll be almost like "déjà vu all over again."

I almost have been many things –
I've been almost smart.
Almost a very good musician.
Almost a farmer.
Almost a student at M.U.

I'm fully grateful for my almost experiences.
For had I been fully smart,
Or fully a very good musician,
Or a farmer,
I might have gone to M.U. or nowhere
And missed meeting Melanie,
And missed the most precious part of life –
Sharing it with the two of you.
I could never almost love you.

Love each other more fully each moment.
I am almost amazed at that ability we have.
Meet each together day fresh as its morning,
Which has fully forgiven the night and history.
Love, Dad

June 4, 2003

At Work
Got to work at about 10:30 local time. Would have been here by 10:00, except for stopping to nap just 8 minutes away, in Abingdon. I didn't sleep worth a darn on the planes. I took a couple of antihistamines to ward off ear pain, and I should have taken just one. I think I made that mistake once before, but forgot the lesson – not apt to do so again. Just took Abby out for a potty break after I got through most of my email. I'm going to do physical stuff the rest of the day. I'm having a munchie lunch – pretzels and trail mix. I'm sipping on hot tea, too. Will have the mowing and trimming to do when I get home. Also quite a lot of mulching left to do – maybe more than we have mulch for.

I feel really good about being useful to you in setting up your place. Of course, none of that work was rocket science, but rocket scientists need their places of sanctuary. One more tool you might want to get is channel-lock pliers. That is the best home tool for working on plumbing, and they operate more easily in more situations than the vice grips. Speaking of plumbing, your new shower head apparatus came complete with thread tape, of which there is a considerable amount left on two blue (?) spools. This keeps threaded pipes from leaking through the threads. If any of your faucets or showerheads is leaky, remove the part at the place whence the leak springeth and wrap more of that tape around the threads. Remember to inspect Venus to be sure that the hanging cable isn't wanting to pull out of its moorings on the back. By the by, I am quite impressed with Anawalt – they have good stuff at reasonable prices, and they were most helpful, from finding what I needed to taking returns with grace, to letting me use their vice, to cutting doors against their usual policy, and for treating me like a valued customer, even though I wasn't a big contractor getting thousands of dollars worth of materials.

It was great to be with you, and to have at least one Nertz session. And it was also terrific to get to help Robbie celebrate his 27th. Just think (please), in a mere four years, Robbie, you will be exactly half my age. Lamelle has to wait six years to be half my age – hmmmm, and she's only a year younger than Robbie.

Work hard and play well. Stay healthy and don't play with knives or matches. Heal quickly from the wounds of adversity. Stretch, walk, and run. Continue to glow and shine.
Love, Dad

To: Larry Rawlins From: Rob Ryman Date: June 4, 2003 Subject: **Re: At Work**
Larry Dean, You are an exquisite work of art! Thank you for the sweet and fun email, and thank you and your wonderful partner for being so generous with time, resources, and spirit! You really should feel good – you launched us on our way. Pard, Jr.

June 13, 2003

Dearest Kids and Granddog,
One of the earliest English language notated songs is the 14th C. round, "*Sumer is icumin in.*"

Sumer is icumen in,
Lhude sing cuccu.
Groweth sed and blweth med,
and springeth the wde nu.
Sing cuccu.
Awe bleteth after lomb,
Lhouth after calve cu.
Bulloc sterteth, bucke verteth,
Murie sing cuccu.
Cuccu, cuccu,
wel singes thu cuccu,
Ne swik thu naver nu.

And we think we speak English. Looks cuckoo to me.

Summer
When seasons come and go in these heartlands,
We adapt to that rhythm of varying light and temperature
And find things to do and places to go
That lift our spirits and delight our senses.
If I were to weep over the passing of a season,
It would be the passing of summer.
Summer makes more things possible,
With its long hours of sun:
The growth of gardens, fields, and blossoms;
Roads free of crystalline accumulations and farm implements;
And vacation time measured in more than weekends.
Living on a tropical island or in southern California
Must have a little of the feel of perpetual summer,
But the tug away from work might be unbearable
In a single-season climate, perhaps ideal for retirement.
Never would I long for winter,
As always I must mourn the passing of summer,
Although, without the perspectives of each season,
How could one really know any other?
Enjoy summer as it comes in, because every day will not feel like summer,
No matter how dearly we hold summer in our hearts;
For every summer day has potential that no winter day can boast.

Rest well in the warmth of your home and hearts.
Love, Dad

~ EVERY FRIDAY: SHABBAT SHALOM FROM A GENTILE FATHER ~

August 8, 2003

Hi Kidz,
I wrote the following in anticipation of other guests. Please accept the invitation for yourselves.

Welcome Guests

We have a nice place in the country:
Lots of trees, shrubs, blossoms, and grasses;
Boat-floating water about an eight iron away;
Lightly traveled paved roads for biking;
Wooded trails for hiking;
Evolving landscape, hospitable to wildlife –
Air-, water-, and land-based
(not to be confused with the U.S. Marine Corps);
Fertile fields of corn and soy;
Near navigable, "gently flowing" river;
World-class sunrises and sunsets;
Clear night skies full of stars and moon;
Such a nice, peaceful place to share.
We look forward to each sharing
With fond anticipation
And just a little frenzied preparation.
Loving the therapeutic thought of having you with us,
Love, Dad

August 15, 2003

Dear Kids,
Basking in the glow of knowing where you live, how you live, and what you live for. So pleased to be a part of your lives. Have fun, rest up, and take care of yourselves and each other. Love, Dad

P.S. Following is a story fragment that spun into my head with the news of the latest suicide bombing in Russia. Could there be possibilities here for a partial solution to that kind of problem?

The Retro

He lay there, unmoving; glazed eyes staring outward to nowhere, as the RRV* - "Arvie" to the team – approached, circled him, sensors alert, then moved closer. To most he appeared dead, but the team monitored rhythmic breathing and a regular pulse via Arvie's sensors. Arvie's "driver" extended the initial probe, which touched the young man's head, and then traversed the length of his body to the toes. A second telescoping probe extended a scalpel-sharp blade toward the supine body, and the tedium of cutting away the clothing, layer by layer, began. As each layer was cut, the first probe pulled the cloth carefully away from the body, until he lay fully exposed in the street just outside the control bunker. Arvie extended two anchors aft and used the first and a third probe to roll the limp, unresponsive body over. There were no alarm beeps from Arvie, there was no explosion, and there was no evidence of explosives. A green light began blinking on Arvie's "head." The team breathed a collective sigh of relief, and Col. Bottomly gave the order for two dispatchers to take the retro man to the infirmary, where he would be revived from the stun blast and given an acceptable wardrobe.

Retros were rare ten months following federal orders to ban loose-fitting, bulky clothing. In the first three nightmarish months following the order there were defiant demonstrations, led by the religious right, and thousands of people were stun blasted into submission. Regular soldiers inspected the fallen masses until the third incident of booby-trapped bodies killed a dozen soldiers and 25 stunned retros. Within a week Arvie, a retrofitted prototype of the old Mars rover, had been equipped with special sensing equipment, transmitters, and cutting hardware. Eventually hundreds of mobile control bunkers were put into service, each with a military team of 4 male and female officers, several enlisted volunteers, and 3 Arvies.

In the year preceding the dress code order, 42 suicide bombing attacks occurred in New York, 31 in Los Angeles, 30 in Chicago, and on and on throughout the contiguous 48. Only Hawaii, Alaska, and the new state of Puerto Rico had been spared. The population of Montana was decimated before federal troops arrived, disarming and arresting most of the survivors.

The process of enforcement was militarily simple. People, soldiers included, were to wear no more than two thicknesses of material in public places; they could wear as little as they wanted, but were to maintain excellent standards of hygiene. Clothing was to be as form fitting as possible. Any deviation sensed by soldiers, Arvies, or surveillance robots – a thin face atop a plump frame, blatant retro-wear, unusual gait, misplaced bulges anywhere – resulted in stun blasting without warning. The effects of the stun blast were immediate, and more than a few medical issues resulted from falling in a heap in mid stride. Recovery from stun blasting was slow but complete. Those who, like the subject above, harbored no weapons or explosives, were resuscitated, given a stern lecture about compliance and the prison term that accompanied repeat offenders, issued some acceptable clothing, and sent on their way. So far there had been no need for enforcer teams to go into people's homes, except in the cases of the few "*sudies*"** who detonated before detection and disarming. Their homes had been searched, family members detained, and neighbors interrogated.

Maybe *Not* The End

*Robotic Reconnaissance Vehicle
**Suicide bombers

~ EVERY FRIDAY: SHABBAT SHALOM FROM A GENTILE FATHER ~

August 22, 2003

Psalm Twenty-free
The school is my employer;
I shall not cry.
It maketh me to sit down with attitudinal kids.
It leadeth me beside the Spoon River.
It restoreth my bank account.
Thou preparest a kosher table before me
For thy name's sake.
Thou annointest my mind with ideas.
My Dong Tam cap runneth them over.
Yea, though I walk through the valley of the sun-parched Spoon,
I will fear no Avon,
For thou art with me.
Thy e-mail and thy cell phone, they comfort me,
And I will dwell in the house of public education until retirement.
Love, Dad

To: Larry Rawlins From: Lamelle & Rob Ryman Date: August 26, 2003 Subject: **Re: ShabbatShvalley**
Dear Abba, Forgot to mention that this was HILARIOUS. I laughed so hard, I cried!!! Wow. Whew. We love you! L (&R in absentia)

August 28, 2003

Want Ad
Love
Knowing
Everything
Necessary
Pusillanimous
Need not apply
Job too tough
Tender
Too

Fly to us tonight,
Be with us tomorrow,
Live in our hearts always.
Love, Dad

September 5, 2003

Being Here...
... and in the air,
the scent of presence,
the feeling of something missing,
though everything's in its place,
and the yearning ear
that waits to hear tones of love
that have vanished, but with a trace
of knowing,
a memory of glowing
at a touch, a laugh, a word,
and, though the beds are remade,
there is the certainty that the love won't fade:
It's in the Post-It notes, in the carpet,
in the yard, in the car,
and in the air...

Shabbat Shalom,
Love, Dad

~ EVERY FRIDAY: SHABBAT SHALOM FROM A GENTILE FATHER ~

September 12, 2003

Shabbat Shtudy Habits

"I must study politics and war, that my sons may have the liberty to study mathematics and philosophy . . . in order to give their children a right to study painting, poetry, music."
John Adams, ca. 1760

If a generation is approximately 25 years, that would be four generations per century. So Adams' children would have studied mathematics and philosophy until about 1785, and their children would have been happily engaged in the arts until about 1810.

So what did the 1810-1835 generation study? War of 1812.

What did the 1835-1880 generation study? Mexican American War, Civil War, gold rush, and Indian Wars.

What did the 1880-1905 generation study? Indian Wars, Spanish American War and westward expansion.

What did the 1905-1930 generation study? $E=MC^2$, World War I, the Great Depression, the fencing in of Native Americans

What did the 1930-1955 generation study? Dust Bowl, World War II, Atom Bomb, Korean War

What did the 1955-1980 generation study? Vietnam War, Cold War, Hydrogen Bomb.

What did the 1980-2005 generation study? Oh.

I probably omitted a skirmish or two.

I will study human nature to understand how we can be so cruel to each other:
How, as a species, we can fail to regard our neighbor as more like us than different;
How we can accept human degradation and carnage as normal or noble.
How we are unable to question our self-righteous assertion of Being.
Shabbat Shalom, Dad

September 19, 2003

The Garden Wall

Soon the garden wall will add its beauty to the homescape,
With wrought iron bench to complement the natural furniture
In this room of leaves and grasses and box elder stump.
Storms like those of this early morning will find no purchase
To dislodge the garden wall from its footings
Next to the Rose of Sharon, oak leaf hydrangea, and wild honeysuckle.
Of course, this wall, like all walls, springs from ulterior motives:
The obverse side, the south, is next to nothing so lovely as the north.
Rather, the wall blushes at its intended purpose –
To hide a very pedestrian tank of propane gas from any who might happen by –
To put on the cloak of something it's not and somehow trick the passersby.
When you pass by, I hope you enjoy the look of it.
Please pass by soon. The wall will be ready.
Love, Dad

September 26, 2003

Shabbat Shjazz

The Annual Al Sears Jazz Festival is this weekend. B-Flat Avenue (that's we) will kick it off. I have the first note of the Festival playing "Don't Get Around Much Anymore" on alto. In addition to our trio – Bill, Darrell, and I – Jim Betts, an unbelievably talented musician and walking encyclopedia of music facts, who is the band guru – a French horn player (!) – at Monmouth College, will be playing his 7-string guitar, and a Macomb High School senior, Bethany Worrell, will sing two tunes, including a credible scat chorus on "Ain't Misbehavin'." Brian Davenport will also be playing harps (harmonicas). Brian doesn't read traditional music, but he has worked out an apparently flawless notation that works for him, but nobody else could follow. He is terrific, showing up at every gig with a toolbox full of "harps." So far as I know, no one will play the *shofar*.

We are having an Al Sears Festival in Macomb, because Al Sears grew up here, then went to NYC and played tenor for Duke Ellington before becoming an influential record producer, especially focusing on black musicians. We are also having a festival because a history professor at WIU, Sterling Kernek, pointed out the connection to Bill Maakestad, our group's organizer and guitarist (a lawyer and professor of business ethics at WIU), and Bill sold the City Council on the idea.

Love and All that Jazz, Dad

October 3, 2003

Awe

Dear Kids,
To be in awe, one must recognize awe for what it is, whether awe-*some* or aw-*ful*. Awe, it seems, is a personal feeling of insignificance in relation to something perceived much larger than oneself. Difficulties may arise in having arrogance enough to deign to be in awe of the awe-some, yet few would doubt universal awe toward the aw-ful. The awe-some is taken for granted: human thought, micro- and macro-life, weather, music, space, sensation, pleasantness, inner peace.... Perhaps *not* inner peace. How can one be in awe of another person's power, *via* their possessions, positions, or accomplishments, without simultaneously coveting the power for oneself? True awe must go beyond the attainable and explainable. True awe must have something to do with Mystery. Does decoding the human genome diminish awe for humanity? Does supersonic flight diminish awe for pedal mobility? Maybe awe is the true nature of prayer. Perhaps awe is evidence of deity in our lives. Or it might just be the wondering.
Love, Dad

October 10, 2003

Dear Kids and Haya,
Hope your Shabbat is shalomish. Thinking about roads:

Roads
All roads lead somewhere, if only to the bogs.
It's good to experience many roads in life –
Land roads, air roads, water roads [space roads?],
Switchbacks, tunnels, dirt, rock, concrete, asphalt,
Creeks, rivers, bays, bayous, seas, channels,
Above the clouds, in fog, stuck, and movin' out.
Follow the road to your somewhere,
And remember your (our) connections along the way.
It's not so important which road is chosen (sorry Mr. Frost);
Much more matters about the traveling companions.
Shabbat Shalom!
Love, Dad

October 21, 2003

Dear Two and Haya,
I am trying to be very quiet at the keyboard, because I have a student here taking a make up Explore test. I would rather give the Explore to the 8th grade, but it is the practice at Valley to test the 9th grade. I have to give the five-minute warning in seven minutes.

Earliest memories of color:
Bright, yellow-white sunrise;
Green car, red tricycle; black tires; white house;
Red, orange, yellow, green, black, and grey tractors; orange combine;
Yellow bananas; orangey oranges; yellow lemons; green beans;
Green grass; blue sky; white, grey, black clouds;
White, black, brownish-grey bark; green leaves; red sun setting;
Pinkish skin; white teeth; blue and brown eyes; red blood;
Redish, brownish, spotted, lacey cattle; black and white hogs;
White and red hens and roosters with red combs and yellow feet;
Brown and white spotted dog.
Grey-black dirt; clear water in white bucket with red bale grip;
Bluish-white milk; black pepper-speckled, white mashed potatoes with
Pale yellow butter and white salt; dark brown coffee;
Yellowed white plates; clear glasses;
Shiny, silvery spoons, forks, and knives;
Blue bib overalls, white underwear, brown shoes, red shirt, blue bandana;

Black, grey, and white smoke from locomotive, cigarette, and bon fire;
Orange flame;
White sheets, blue blankets, multi colored quilted comforters;
Rainbow dreams; spectral sleep.
Shabbat Shalom,
Love, Dad

To: Larry Rawlins From: Lamelle & Rob Ryman Date: October 21, 2003 Subject: **Color**
Hello, Papa. This is beautiful! Amazing how calling up all of those images in quick succession can add such color and vibrancy to the span of a few moments. Awesome. I love you sooooo much. Lamelle Daile Rawlins Ryman

October 31, 2003

Shabbat Shpooky Shbirthday

Dear Kids and, especially, Haya,
It's Halloween.
It's also Abby's second birthday.
Seems like only yesterday that she was a tiny puppy, unable to climb even a single stair step, precariously slipping over snow mounds at 3:00 a.m. Now she not only sleeps through the night, but she serves as the backup alarm clock – creature of habit that she is – although her internal clock has yet to adjust to CST.

I've been training her slowly and undeliberately to sit, stay, lie down, roll over – the usual stuff. But what I'm most proud of is her prowess in making breakfast. Her golden pancakes with maple syrup, freshly squeezed OJ, and freshly ground coffee are the best ever. Yes she's come a long way in just 2 human years.

If a dog's year is 7 of humans' years, then she is at the age of flowering adolescence – capable, but unpredictably moody. Thus attuned to her developmental needs, it has been possible to make astonishing progress with her training.

Some dogs learn to fetch their masters' slippers. Abby has no time for such foolishness, because she is busy laying out a coordinated wardrobe for Mom and me. Don't ever let someone tell you that dogs are colorblind. Abby has never suggested garish or clashing colors, and her taste in ties is impeccable. She is rather over-fond of one particular bra, which Mom wears on occasion so as not to hurt Abby's feelings. The relatively fleeting discomfort of distended stays is but nothing compared to the potential for psychological torment of rejection.

Since Abby spends most of her daytime alone in the utility room, she often has the laundry done – and pressed! – when we arrive home. She is such a good girl. I don't think that many adolescent human daughters or sons would be so thoughtful (perhaps if they were locked up . . . ?).

I must admit to a flight of nervousness with the realization that in a few months she will expect to drive. Her independence may be more than we can bear, and the anticipated worry is frightful. But how does one deny anything in the face of such precociousness and loyalty. That she is insufferably cute and cuddly only fans the flames of utter spoilage.

Just last night, when we were dining by candlelight on one of Abby's original recipes, I remarked to my remarkable spouse that there is something about Abby that is just special. I suppose other dogged families feel the same about their canine adoptees, but I just have a sense, however irrational and exuberant, that Abby is, you know, like, out there!

We had Snoopy from next-door, over for a fourth for Nertz a few weeks ago. Well, to tell the truth, she couldn't even hold her cards, let alone go through them. What a disappointment! And she is much older than Abby. Perhaps Abby *is* precocious, or maybe that's simply what happens in households with satellite TV permanently tuned to ESPN. I'm afraid that some pets are just left behind, through no fault of their own, of course.

The primary problem we have is with communication. While Abby has learned to respond to an amazing variety of human verbiage, we have yet to learn much in the way of *Caniniano*. But we tend to get by O.K. with a kind of *Doglish*, attended by useful gestures. But sometimes it can get embarrassing. Late one night I remarked, in my doggutteral way, that it was bedtime, only to realize that I had improperly nuanced a syllable, and Abby went, insulted and sulking, to her crate in the closet. I finally coaxed her out with much apologizing, promising to do better in the future.

No matter what, I know that she'll be glad to see us when we get home tonight. She is so glad to have a night off from cooking! And, of course, there will be a cake and two candles.

Happy Birhday, Dear Abby, Happy Birthday to You (and many more).
Now, make a wish . . .

Shabbat Shalom,
Love, Dad

November 7, 2003

If I Had My Life to Live Over
I had heard the attached ("If I Had My Life to Live Over") before, then heard it on the way from Valley to Avon on NPR's 51% program. I think Erma Bombeck wrote it after being diagnosed with a terminal illness.

Just a Step
That there be no lament for life unfulfilled,
That there be flowers and rainbows in mind
Instead of weeds and storms,
That there be joyful recollections,
That there be reasons for reunions,
That there be moments to celebrate
And people to venerate,
That we might know soul-caressing touch,
That there be tolerance of differences
And acceptance of common ground,
I would take a right step today
And carefully consider tomorrow's stride.
Shabbat Shalom
Love, Dad

To: Larry Rawlins
From: Lamelle Ryman
Date: November 7, 2003
Subject: Erma and You
Dear Abba,
Erma Bombeck's piece was spectacular. Yours was, too, as always!!! Thank you!!!
I can't wait to see you and get your blessing in person this Shabbat. ☺
Loads of love, L

~ EVERY FRIDAY: SHABBAT SHALOM FROM A GENTILE FATHER ~

November 21, 2003

The View from Hear
A boy, 15, near-deaf,
Angry because others laugh.
Mistaking others' mirthful moments
For directed derision and cruelty.
No way to argue with the perception,
No way to cause others to change;
Now a yearning to protect,
But from what?
To hear 85% with eyes,
Suspicious of motives behind smiles,
Feeling unloved and abandoned,
Because of having been unloved and abandoned;

He meets his mother tomorrow –
First time in twelve years.
Where will the anger go?
How will his eyes hear excuses?
Suspicion borne by history,
Anger bent on harm.
How will his eye shear and shred
The fear, the dread?

Inside a mostly silent body,
How will he break out
Into a friendly world
That cares and sustains?
Spare some love for him, anyone?
Might save a soul
Or, at least, a life.
Spare some love and feel it return.
Love, Dad

December 1, 2003

End of the Day
Dear Kids,
Had a ball,
That's not all,
Ridin' tall,
Thinkin' small,
Time to call
It a day.

Love, Dad

December 5, 2003

ShabbatShwonder

Dearest Adult Children,

Wonder hangs right in there with awe as the mysterious sensation, near fear, which invites personal humility before the natural domino effects of dizygotic processes. At this fresh moment, not to possess wonder or awe would be unthinking and unthinkable.

I pride myself on never giving advice. Following is some of the advice you're not getting, because I never give it:

0. First, do no harm.
1. Work, and save for college – yours.
2. Remember to put the cap on the toothpaste
3. Buy absolutely *everything* you *need*.
4. Turn off lights you aren't using.
5. Ask for what you want, but don't blame me if you get it.
6. Regular auto maintenance can save your car and your lives.
7. Keep your pants properly on in public.
8. Remember that living is the primary responsibility of life.
9. Eat absolutely *everything* you *need*.
10. Indulge unharmful fantasies.

Ten – or was that eleven? – are probably enough pieces of advice *not* to give at one time, but here are a few more, anyway: Never take advice; if you hear about an idea that is appealing, adopt it and immediately forget where it came from, except in the cases of copyright/patent-protected information/devices – always give credit and avoid debt.

15? Hang in there. On occasion, hang out here.
Shabbat Shalom.
Love, Dad

To: Larry Rawlins
From: Lamelle & Rob Ryman
Date: December 5, 2003
Subject: **Advice**
Dear Papa, This time I couldn't resist "peeking" before candlelighting! Thank you for this beautiful, fun and amusing piece. I would take your advice anytime. It's true that as long as I can remember, you haven't made a habit of giving out advice to me, but I readily welcome your shared wisdom. In fact, earlier this week, I was reflecting on how much I treasure the "Elf Help" book that you gave me several years ago. I love reading and re-reading it and imagining you as the Elf. I love you sooooo much, and Robbie joins me in wishing you and Mom a wonderful weekend! Xoxoxox ldr

December 12, 2003

My Place
Ramble along with me on the Avon *Rambla*. Smell and taste the coffee, kept warm and fragrant on the desktop mug warmer, in a cup rarely empty or washed. See the sights – the new "mural" on the opposite wall – triangles, squares, and rectangles in green, gray, and black on a snow-white background. See the wildlife from my very own mouse nest behind the cabinets. Hear the class next door get so loud that hearing aids become a detriment. Feel the oppressive heat of an antiquated heating system that never knew balance. Peruse the library of a hundred volumes on curriculum, counseling, and music. Rifle through six file cabinets full of test materials, temporary records, ICPs, conference notes, and collected articles. Wash your hands at the double sink and dry them with paper towels. Select a video on any of scores of careers. Become inspired from the bulletin board dressed in posters proclaiming that the last 12 years of public education are less important than the first year (thanx to Mr. Fulghum), the message of the little train that could (sans train), a precious child's artwork, photos of memories, and information focusing on the future. The floor still shines, even through the dust that didn't succumb to the custodian's broom. The Boston pencil sharpener is rarely used, because there is an electric on the desk. And, of course, the computer and printer, purveyors of information, advertising, and moments like these, loom always in the foreground until a student walks in. And the photo of a young woman and young man, her left arm arced around his neck, left hand draped over his left shoulder at the seven o'clock position below his chin, right hand holding two fingers of the left, faces smiling confidence, radiating the future – a small photo in gold and burgundy frame – is the focal point of all points.
Shabbat Shalom,
Love, Dad

To: Larry Rawlins
From: Lamelle & Rob Ryman
Date: December 12, 2003
Subject: **Re: My Place**
Dear Abba,
What an incredible experience to read your words and imagine each image, each sensation in my mind's/heart's eye. It was hauntingly beautiful even as you described the most mundane elements of your environment. Thank you for the precious, deliciously unexpected ending.
I love you, ldr

December 19, 2003
Dear Ones,
I'm about to close up shop for the holidays. I feel good about the condition of the
room. It's neatened up nicely, so I'll feel good about getting back to it on January
8. Jan. 5,6,7 are Valley Dayze. I love you deeply. Happy Holidays. Please convey our love and best wishes to the Hyman/Kammerman families; we know this is a tough time for all. Breathe sweetly.
Love, Dad

2004 ✡ 5764

~2004~

January 9, 2004

Time

We saw *Return of the King* last night, but the audio in that theater is so awful, that neither of us could catch most of the dialogue. Interesting preview of a movie, which name has slipped to the nether reaches of memory. It is about someone who has figured out how to go forward and backward in time, so he tries to manipulate fate, or something like that. Coincidentally, there was a NYT article on the nature of time - one of my 70 + emails waiting after the holidays (I just finished putting the last one to bed).

Time Foreseen
Always time:
Perspective's important.
Analogue's more accurate than digital.
What would *you* tell time if you could?
Speeding with time slows it down.
Sitting on the edge of a black hole slows time more.
It would be ever so interesting to go away for a while
And return 9,000 years later; maybe someone already will.
Remember the movie, "Awakenings"?
And "Groundhog Day"? Oh, for the chance to get one day right!
I like Kurt Vonnegut, Jr.'s notion of becoming unstuck in time;
Like conventional time is some kind of glue imprisoning us in 2 or 3 dimensions,
When there are really infinite convolutions in the time-space continuum
Offering us infinite potentialities of temporal presence and progress.
Then there is the Desiderata ("*Go* [now] . . . ." "*You may become . . .*"
". . . *always there will be. . . .*" ". . . *changing fortunes of time.*"
". . . *counsel of the years. . . surrendering the things of youth.*"
". . . *be . . . .*" ". . . *broken dreams . . . .*").
Before that was the Sanskrit proverb: ". . . *today, well-lived,*
Makes every yesterday a dream of happiness
And every tomorrow a vision of hope."
What will be the next great time event?
What, about time, will be greatly remembered?
I think it was time spent with others in both instances,
Not super-accelerated particles crashing at Fermi.
With care and planning, this day will be but a prelude
To times when we can look to those days
As the "life of life," never looking at a clock or calendar,
And creating a Heaven of memories on Earth.
As *always*,
Love, Dad

~ EVERY FRIDAY: SHABBAT SHALOM FROM A GENTILE FATHER ~

January 16, 2004

Shabbat Shvacuum

Hi kids,

I am about to order the Oreck XL 3700 vac. for our cleaning pleasure. It is hypo-allergenic, weighs just 8 lbs., has an endorsement from the Arthritis Foundation, has a 5 year motor warranty, has no leaky attachments on the upright - Instead, it comes with a separate canister vac with attachments. With our 28 carpeted stairs, the lightness is a major enticement; our current Hoover is *troppo pesante* at best. We also have plenty of space for storing the canister vac. And the owner of Floor to Ceiling, where we bought a couple of our good rugs, has one and likes it. (This piece is not an endorsement) So let's think about vacuums:

Vacuum

Absence, emptiness,
Dearth, void,
Nothing, null,
Nihilism, extinction,
Oblivion, rarefaction,
Nonexistence. . .
There is nothing so *not there* or *here* as vacuum.
There is nothing so *nothing*.
And yet nothing else is quite so powerful toward everything around its nothingness.
Vacuum is the primary ingredient in system change.
Without some sense of void, there is only equilibrium, a lack of motivation.
But create a vacuum next to an idea, and watch that idea get pushed into the void.
There is nothing more compelling for Y as the absence of X.
With that in mind, how is it possible that the vacuous mental meanderings of Politicians can withstand the scrutiny of substantive ideas and ideals?
Could it be the theory of vacuous relativity - $E = MC/0$, where E is Enactment, M is Maintenance, C is Challenge, and 0 is zero, and so is everything else?
Some zeros are just more *zero* than others - think Animal Farm.
To make positive changes in the world,
Create strategic vacuums next to only the best alternatives.
It isn't necessary to understand what is missing
As long as there is something useful to fill the space.
This has been known by good salespeople forever - think Harold Hill.
In life we can ask for what we want whether we are suffering from its lack or not.
Of course, it's still prudent to be careful what you ask for.

The weekend, Shabbat, holidays, and retirement are examples of vacuums,
Which cause us to be compelled to behave differently than we do during work-days/years. Let's consider carefully what we would place next to the void, because that's what will fill it.

Love, Dad

To: Larry Rawlins From: Lamelle Ryman Date: January 16, 2004 Subject: **Re: Vacuum**
Dear Dad, This is a beautiful one. I found that it resonated with some of my feelings about the miscarriage, the quintessential "emptiness". I can elaborate; if you're interested, ask me. I love you. Have a great weekend! love you, L

To: Lamelle & Rob Ryman From: Larry Rawlins Date: January 16, 2004 Subject: **Re: Vacuum**
Dear Lamelle, Please elaborate. Love, Dad

January 23, 2004

Fable Rethought

There's a crack in the wall near the door,
And I don't recall seeing it before.
Buildings settle, and warp and bend concrete to shapes builders don't intend.
It's the old fable in new clothes, of trees like oaks and willows,
Standing against the stormy wind,
To find that ever in the end
The oak that fights the most is uprooted from its post
While supple willows stand, roots still clinging to the land.
The broken wall has weathered storms, and sheltered many different forms
Of body, mind, spirit, heart - each one here to have a part
In choosing the sort of tree to be -
The kind that fall or those that see the sunrise after dark,
Harboring the singing lark.
The wall will one day break entire,
Succumb to demolition's fire,
But those bodies, minds, spirits, hearts,
That learned here, left here, got their starts,
Will build more shelters, plant more trees,
To stand against wind and thaw and freeze.
And supple souls again will win
Midst the awesome, stormy din.
Love, Dad

~ EVERY FRIDAY: SHABBAT SHALOM FROM A GENTILE FATHER ~

January 30, 2004

Mountain Top Experience

Can you see the mountain?
Is the smog too dark, too thick?
Can you hear the tale was told before the world got sick?
Can you feel the passion?
Is the fire still there?
Can you smell the smoke that billows from the bombs somewhere?
Go tell about the mountain;
It's disappeared from view.
Let everyone remember; especially you.
Go tell about the bombs;
They're everywhere tonight.
No one's safe or out of danger 'til the world gets right;
Not just over there,
But here and all around,
Exploding in the morning -
Can't you hear that sound?
All the weeping, ripping, anguish,
For lost brother, mother, friend;
World on fire - a cold quagmire;
For everyone, the end
Of what we knew as normal -
What we thought was true.
Look toward the mountain
For what saves me and you.
But who can see the mountain
Through this cruel, smoggy haze?
It may not really be there;
Who knows how long it stays?
But if the fire still burns within
To make this world your home,
Don't wait until it comes to you;
To the mountain you must roam.
And tell the foggy, smoggy folk
Below of what you see;
And reassure the queens and drones
That workers set them free.
And let the smog and fog recede
To caverns far below
So all might see the mountain
And to the mountain all may go.
Love and Peace, Dad

February 6, 2004

Hi Kidz

Congratulations on selling your car so quickly. Don't have your head in the clouds as you drive among the stars. Be safe and save us a seat.

Car Talk

Glad that you could sell the Ford in such a timely fashion.
Selling things of any kind has never been my passion.
Hope your Camry proves to be the best of all used cars.
Drive it safely every day 'round rich and famous film stars.
Over mountain, hill, and dale, in all the city traffic,
Pay attention to the laws – the nat'ral and the graphic.
Happy wheelz to you.
Shabbat Shalom, Dad

To: Larry Rawlins From: Lamelle & Rob Ryman Date: February 6, 2004 Subject: **Re: Car Talk**
Thank you, Abba!!!! Yep, it is a big relief! And the Camry seems to be terrific so far. Thank you for your good wishes -- we look forward to the time when you're riding in our Camry. Safe driving to you -- o ye of resplendent wintertide. Love and warmth -- happy V-day, L&R

~ EVERY FRIDAY: SHABBAT SHALOM FROM A GENTILE FATHER ~

February 13, 2004

Shabbat ShValentine
Determine first reader, first listener. Take turns.
Sit down. Sit up straight with your hands resting on your thighs.
Close your eyes if you wish, and take a deep breath through your nose.
Exhale it slowly through your lips.
Feel the weight of your body increase
As you let go of every vain effort to control gravity.
Inhale. . . exhale.
Feel the tug at your center,
Being pulled toward the core of Earth
While simultaneously suspended weightless in space,
In perfect balance between forces.
Enjoy the view inside your mind
As it takes in everything it needs
To assure your comfort and safety.
Listen to the wisdom of silence.
As thoughts spring, wordless, to life, at the speed of light,
Feel the peace that comes from knowing without remembering.
Anticipate the ease with which things future, *now* are fixed in progress.
Welcome any sense of ambivalence as proof of congruity.
Breathe in . . . breathe out. Breath reassures the mind.
Surprise yourself by noticing tingling or numbness somewhere,
And focus on that place as long as you need to be sure about . . .
Now, . . . as the voice with these words grows distant,
Feel how much heavier one hand feels than the other,
Like the light hand has a helium balloon attached
And the heavy hand is like lead.
And it really doesn't matter that there are world-sounds around you.
(Extended quiet)
You don't have to notice what happens, and you may be surprised
As you become aware of a force lifting one hand toward your face,
While the other is weighted down too much to move anywhere but down.
(Extended quiet)
I don't know what things will seem clearer to you now than before,
But as sure as there is any difference between left and right, there will be clarity.
Now become aware again of the sounds of the world outside.
Notice how your hands are beginning to feel their equitable weight.
Let each hand discover its own pace and path,
And, as they get closer to their resting places,
Open your eyes and look around at the
Reassuring friendliness and safety of this place in this time.
Notice what seems the same and what seems different.
Share observations with each other.
Happy Valentine's Day, Dad

February 20, 2004

Dearest Kids,
This morning's musings:

Teases Pleases

The Mother of All Nature is in full tease today.
The calendar confirms the season winter,
Yet rain is in the February forecast, not snow,
And no one has heard such happy birds
As those that sang during Abby's morning walk.
Still cold by coastal standards,
It's been a while since temps in the 50s,
And, here, that feels good.
Seasonal affective disorder has no purchase.
Because it's just a tease,
We must take care not to take too seriously
The balminess and hopeful birdsong.
We shall shovel yet more snow before
Dr. Cobb's daffodils bloom golden.
But today is Spring;
I'm clearly told by the reddest of cardinals,
Who never sings blues.
So happy spring to all!
Happy melting, Snow!
Soak into needy soil and run to lakes and streams
To refresh fish, float boats, and return through faucets.
"The world is a circle without a beginning,
And nobody knows where the circle ends. . . ." *
The cycle of life is amazing!
With only one trip around we are compelled, now,
To take care of what we have, now,
To prepare with a faith-driven certainty
For a future that can't be certain.
How rational is that?
How rational is that cardinal?
Let's celebrate today's "irrational exuberance,"
And feel glad to be alive and to have each other.
Buon Primavera!
Love, Dad

(Bacharach/David)

~ EVERY FRIDAY: SHABBAT SHALOM FROM A GENTILE FATHER ~

February 27, 2004

Hi Kidz,

It's petting zoo day at AHS, and the action is all next door - two ponies, a couple of dogs, two lambs, a maternal goat and her kid, one large white rat, some exotic chickens - easily discernable species. Having the Event next to me also means there is a parade of elementary students back and forth in the hall, so for today I have my door closed, but unlocked. Soon I must get back to triple checking the senior transcripts for graduation deficiencies. At this point, if anyone is missing a necessary class, I may just pony up for their tuition for a correspondence course; with luck, the only ponies are in our zoo. The following is inspired by an internet story.

The M&M Connection
Scientific reports are now published about advantages of the M&M shape over the shape of balls. It seems that flattened particles can touch twice the number of adjacent surfaces as round ones, thereby making surfaces, materials, and structures much stronger. I don't exactly understand the physics of this engineering principle, but I understand M&Ms. Pound for pound they take up less space on the store shelf but add much more waistline than jaw breakers, which last much longer. Neither is particularly good for teeth, but only the second possesses the potential for acute dental catastrophe. There is something infinitely more soothing and satisfying about M&Ms over, say, gumballs; I'm sure, now, that's due to the shape. During my early childhood, before M&Ms had been invented, I made my own observations about shape. My mother, who was a very round woman, was also very soft and snuggly; whereas my father, who was thin, sinewy, and bony, was less so. Although I lacked the proper vocabulary at age 1 1/2, I reasoned that concave - the shape that results when sinking into something soft - was cushier than convex - witness pillows, mattresses, and mothers. Later, I learned idiomatic phrases, such as, " the shape of things to come." I was always much aware of "the shape of things to *go*," because we had a car, tractors, and so forth, which *went*. By the time I could envision the shapes of things to come, they were already here. *The shape of things to come* became confused in other idioms, such as "*second coming*," and so on. By the time I could envision the second coming, Hollywood had killed Him again*. In the beginning, the earth was without form and void; this is also the likely shape of things to come, unless those, who believe that they were created in the image of the creator accept their own humanity and identify more with the rest of us terrestrials, whom they can see, instead of with God, who remains a mystery. Although our diversity is partly a diversity of shapes, we are nonetheless more alike than different. Put us in cages and keep us in zoos, and the ET visitor would be hard put to tell us apart, except for male and female. Why do we have so much trouble with that, ourselves? Maybe we should all be shaped like M&Ms, able to touch and be touched by a dozen neighbors at once. Maybe then we'd treat more of our neighbors like family, and our shells would be colorful, thin, and sweet.

Love, Dad

*Mel Gibson's "The Passion of Christ," which was wildly successful and troublingly anti-semitic.

March 5, 2004

Shabbat Shwind

March winds and April showers bring May flowers.
If the April showers of this spring are in proportion to the present March winds, we will be potting the petunias of May in an Ark. The resident robins and migrating honkers must hunker down tonight, as temps are expected to plummet and snow may return as the prevailing precipitation. I still don't think I'd mind living in a climate a bit less volatile and more moderate.

There is music in the hall. A boom box is booming some city man's country voice. For no apparent reason, I am remembering a T.V. special from the early 60s. The main star was Sammy Davis, Jr. I haven't a clue who the other actors were, but the basic story line has stayed with me. In my fallible memory, it goes something like this:

*Once upon a time a white boy and a black boy were childhood chums. They remained friends through school, one doing typical middle class white boy things and Sam helping to augment his family's livelihood by shining shoes; after graduation they went their separate ways and lost contact. Years later, the two adults met by chance when the white adult [let's call him Jim] was dining with his wife [Jane] in a very upscale restaurant. Jim and Sam were thrilled to see each other. Jim assumed that Sam worked at the restaurant, and Sam allowed that to be true, except Sam explained that he **owned** the restaurant. Jim was astonished that Sam – or maybe inwardly he was thinking "Sambo" - could be the owner of such a posh establishment. Jim and Jane were delighted for Sam, and they agreed to meet again to get caught up on their lives. Some time before their scheduled rendezvous Jim and Jane decided to have dinner at Sam's restaurant again. As they rounded a corner they were thunderstruck to see Sam busy on the opposite corner shining shoes! Jim and Jane assumed that Sam had lied to them about owning the restaurant, and, not wanting to embarrass Sam [or themselves], they made a hasty retreat without saying anything to him. Jim was troubled by this revelation, so he decided to confront Sam about it. He went to Sam and asked him why he had lied and put on such a front about owning the restaurant. Sam explained the circumstances: He **did** own the restaurant, and was quite rich. However, he was determined never to forget where he had come from and what it was like to be poor. Therefore, every [Friday?] he got out his shoeshine gear and took to the street like the old days.*

I guess the moral of the story is something like, "No matter how far you've come, you came from somewhere, and that's important to remember." Neither of you were privileged to know my parents. I think the most honest snapshot of them is the one I took by the "front" door to the Amity farmhouse – Dad in his overalls and Mom in a faded cotton dress –which photo we keep on the "secretary" in the antique room. That scene and the dirt, creek, crops, and animals of the farm are where I'm from – Mom's "past-somewhere" is similar – and I like to remember it occasionally.
Love, Dad

~ EVERY FRIDAY: SHABBAT SHALOM FROM A GENTILE FATHER ~

March 12, 2004

Shabbat Shjoint
We continue to enjoy the Joint gig recordings. Mom took the CD with her this morning for traveling music. I think you should target Ryman Hall in Nashville as a future venue. It's "institute day" at school today, so the kids get the day off. We were just told that we can leave at 2:00. *Hasta La Vista.*
Love, Dad

March 19, 2004

Car Talk II
Imagine, if you will, 4,000 years ago
In some Middle Eastern or Chinese shops,
Customers browsing through the latest
Innovations in sandals and camel saddles.
What would be the pitch?
One is easy on your toes the other on your tush?
And all in the latest fashion to impress the neighbors,
With the latest prices to match the demand.
Then, somewhere on the plains of Spain
Someone saddled a fiery steed
And started a revolution in travel and warfare.
And everyone wanted one of those
Broken to ride, broken to pull,
Broken-to-human-will *caballos*.
Things went along like that for a long time,
Then, some time after Roman war chariots,
Humans started messing around
With combustible locomotion -
At first water steamed by wood or coal, then
The Internal Combustion Engine,
Horseless (!) carriages,
Airplanes, and Model Ts.
Life was simpler before -
Repair the sole of the sandal,
Fix the cinch of the saddle,
Mend the wheel of the wagon -
Tasks easily taken on at home.
There always were people who would help
When the work was perplexing;
We call them mechanics now.
Mechanics were the people
Who put more straw in the sole of the sandal,
Replaced worn leather on the saddle,

Put spokes back in the wagon wheel, and
Charged people enough to make a living.
Now, our society is largely post-walking,
Even though the sole technology is at its zenith.
We are also post-equestrian, except as a hobby,
Although horse breeding is a flourishing business.
We *need* our horseless carriages
And featherless flying machines
To maintain our global economy
And get us to the gym for our workouts.
And, because "necessity never made a good bargain",
According to Ben Jamin Franklin,
We often pay the mechanic and the salesperson
At least enough for them to make a living.
Living is a good thing for everyone.
Love, Dad

~ EVERY FRIDAY: SHABBAT SHALOM FROM A GENTILE FATHER ~

March 26, 2004

It's teenybopper time in the Midwest,
That "twixt 12 and 20" time
Of fields fresh-tilled, *sans* growth;
Lawns not quite green, not quite brown;
Trees with almost-leaves;
Gray skies without snow;
Finished with a fine March wind,
Apparently trying to blow us straight into June.
Temperamental and sometimes scary,
The air supersaturated,
The last trimester of March
Invokes its successor with occasional torrents.
As with all adolescents,
This is a time of promise and expectations:
The signs of the first are obvious;
Of the second we must look inward,
Then deal with the match/mismatch to reality.
The pelicans on the lake are temporary distractions,
As are the sea gulls that follow the thaw
To harvest Winter's fish-kill from inland waters.
We've seen but one bald eagle so far.
Being an adolescent time,
We expect excesses -
Too much rain, wind, and lightning;
Too much growth of the lawn;
Too much the siren song
To play hooky and golf during sunny interludes.
And, always, the sense, the promise,
That summer can't be far behind.
Shabbat Shalom,
Love, Dad
P.S. I think we are thinking L.A. in June.

To: Larry Rawlins	
From: Lamelle & Rob Ryman	
Date: March 26, 2004	
Subject: **Re: Shabbat ShMarching Orders**	
Haven't read your poem/blessing yet, because it ain't Shabbat yet... but i did scroll down and see the p.s. -- shucks. Does that mean no LA for Easter? Oh well. I was getting psyched to see you guys now and then. Maybe we'll try to come to Macomb in June. L&R	

April 8, 2004

Hello California,

Since we'll be gone tomorrow, tho't I'd drop a line today, especially since we were gone last Friday.

Gotta Start Somewhere

To drop a line I've never held before,
To hold a thought that hands can never touch,
To reach another's soul with songs and such:
My Quest on this or other distant shore.

To feel the pain of those whom we would love,
To love someone so much it seems to hurt,
Absorbing feelings dragged through thorns and dirt:
This, too, my quest, at last, would be thereof.

To live perchance. . ., in spite . . ., in faithful daze?
To have a purpose: Better in a haze
Than blind meanderings through darkness groped,
And ever better off than we had hoped,

Before the truth shone through with golden rays
To shine sad light on ways we'd often coped,
So ever after choices better made,
And ever after never more afraid.

Shabbat Shpassover, Dad

To: Larry Rawlins
From: Lamelle & Rob Ryman
Date: April 11, 2004
Subject: **Re: Gotta Start Somewhere**
BEAUTIFUL....
Thank you so much for this…
We love you!
Happy Easter, happy Spring, happy Love.
L&R

~ EVERY FRIDAY: SHABBAT SHALOM FROM A GENTILE FATHER ~

April 16, 2004

Hi Kids,
Your Passover with the NYC folks seemed to have all of the memorable elements - Things that went well, things that went funny, and time that just went wanting (more). Thanks for sharing Sy's poignant messages to you and Kent and Ginny.

We have the UU in for TGIF this evening, beginning at 5:30. We expect low numbers. Donna Phillips' retirement party is at 4:00, so we hope to be on time for our own party. We expect L.A. weather today - high 85, no smog, but considerable field dust in the air (farmers are frantically disking and planting in anticipation of next week's promised rain).

Mom said that Robbie is getting into the post-bacc game, too, and that Lamelle has given up one position. Good luck to all.

Shabbat ShUnderstanding
"Understand" is a funny word.
Under stand: Is it a fruit stand, a lemonade stand, or what?
And why would anyone want to stand under one?
To *take* a stand, be it fruit or lemonade or other, might make better sense.
If one takes a stand, then gets under it to support it, I suppose understanding occurs.
In the past couple of days, Mom and I have called our IL and US legislators in an effort
To help them understand that, if they don't support some stands we take,
They will cease to be rewarded by our votes
(This is applicable to three of the four).
Then there are times when understanding just isn't necessary.
I don't need to understand an illness to empathize the suffering it brings.
I don't have to understand Judaism to love my children.
Then there's that phrase: "The peace that passeth all understanding," I remember it goes.
There are times when it isn't necessary to ask why or how.
Those times are the ones when we accept what seems to be reality and move on.
Aging comes to mind, as "moving on" takes on changing connotations.
It has been written: "Dust to dust. . . ." I prefer to think of it as "Love to Love."
You understand, don't you?
Love, Dad

April 23, 2004

Dear Family,
It's been quite a while since I've been a real lame duck in a job. The distancing from staff at Valley, and my own emotional distancing, create a strange, eerie climate in which to work. The atmosphere at Avon, paradoxically, has been a bit better in recent days. Go figure. I've been wanting to write about the people of my childhood, so I'm going to attempt that below.

Strange Happenings
Earlier this week, I had to go to Avon in the morning, then to Valley. Since I had my lunch with me, I stopped at London Mills - the post office address of Valley school - and parked in the boat launch area next to the Spoon River to have my contracted 30-minute duty-free lunch. While driving through LM, I saw a house that evoked memories from Amity days. It was a single story, probably about 5 rooms, house that was apparently being painted, changing its color from white to blue or blue to white. The painting work was about half completed, and both white and blue looked oldish, so it was difficult to tell which color was new. Regardless, the house looked exactly like Clayton and Verneda Dishman's house, which was always being painted, never finished.

Clayton and Verneda lived one half mile north and one mile west of our Amity, Missouri, farmhouse; they had no children. They farmed small acreage, some of the worst soil and terrain in DeKalb County, including Little Third Fork Creek bottom that flooded every spring, ditches, and steep, rocky hills.

Clayton's overt character was stereotypical southern redneck, happy-go-lucky, and irreligious. He was younger than Dad, but always had less hair and a potbelly. Clayton supplemented their crop and livestock income by bailing hay for the neighbors, charging 1 - 2 cents per 50-pound bale. His best tractor was a Farmall "C" (a size smaller than our "H"), and it, like the baler, was often broken down. He also had a John Deere - one of the older models that had to be started by turning the flywheel by hand. That was the first tractor I drove as part of a hay crew, when I was 9 years old.

Verneda had the twangiest Missouri ("muzurruh") twang I ever heard. She was loud, like Clayton, and I couldn't imagine her ever looking pretty. She became a devout member of the Reorganized Church of Jesus Christ of Latter Day Saints (RLDS) - the branch of Mormons still centered in Independence, Mo., instead of having traveled on to Utah. We went to some "meetin's" and services in Maysville with them. I occasionally sang solos there, accompanied by a talented, blind pianist. On the farm Verneda took care of the chickens, eggs, and milk, and she helped out with the livestock and other farm and fieldwork more than my mother.

At all times Clayton and Verneda had time to talk or help, and her kitchen always kept a welcoming cup of coffee. However, even as a child I had disdain for vulgarity and the kind of overbearing, good grammarless speech, which marked that part of northwest Missouri. I felt somehow superior to the Dishmans, if only because my family and I could speak the language, and that I, unlike Clayton, could speak without cursing. That Dad cursed about the unfinished paint job didn't help my immature attitude. Since Clayton and Verneda offered me no childhood playmates during our visits, I was generally bored and made myself scarce.

One evening, with our living room full of neighbors, with Dad fiddling an Irish jig to Mom's three-chord piano second, and old Tom Gibson magically dancing to the music with a corner of the carpet turned back, a strange thing happened: Clayton asked for dad's fiddle. He said that he hadn't played for many years, but he'd like to give it a try. He played another jig, and a couple of other stalwarts of the country fiddlers' repertoire, and he sounded almost as good as Dad! Thereafter, I felt closer and kindlier toward the Dishmans. Before that evening I had no idea that Clayton was such a cultured gentleman.

We have met the judge and s/he is us.
Love, Dad

To: Larry Rawlins
From: Lamelle Ryman
Date: April 30, 2004
Subject: **Re: Shabbat Shought**

What a beautiful, vivid, captivating reflection to add to the *New Spoon River Anthology/Theology/Pathology/Psychology* (I'm just trying out book titles).

Did you see my article yet?!?!?!?! www.jewishjournal.com Cover story!!!
Love, ldr

To: Lamelle & Rob Ryman
From: Larry Rawlins
Date: April 30, 2004
Subject: **Re: Shabbat Shought**

Hi,
Thanks for your feedback. Pathology?!?!?
Read your article with great interest, respect, love and pride. We'll probably be seeing more Lamelle cover stories through the years. This is an incredibly auspicious beginning.
Love, Dad

May 7, 2004   **Shabbat Shpaper**

When I was in grade school *My Weekly Reader*, which is still around as paper journalism for kids, came out with a futuristic story about a world, some day, when there would be no more need for consumers to carry paper money. Transactions of that future would be handled with a small plastic card. That sounded absurd; none of us in the class could imagine such a thing. Yet here we are in the plastic money age; and plastic buys debits and credits in most amounts in most venues. Of course, the Treasury continues to print money on paper, and people continue to carry currency, and we insist on paper receipts for our plastic transactions.

There is great power in paper. Even in the old "1,2,3" game, paper is a winner when it covers rock. Hornets, homeless people, and the Japanese use it in the construction of dwellings. Most Americans merely decorate their walls with it.

Imagine how the first paper must have been received. Here was a medium for record keeping, art, communication, and trade that had to be more convenient than rocks, drums, and shells. It was made from renewable resources, trees or grain, and spawned new technologies in ink, paint, points, and brushes. Most important: It was portable. The reader of history didn't have to travel to the cave or pyramid or obelisk; rather the message could be delivered by some kid on a bicycle, if, simultaneously, bicycles had been invented, which they weren't. I'll bet that there was a bunch of stone-chipping old farts hanging around the barbershop declaring this weak, crumbling burnable stuff to be a faddish blip in history.

Many blips later, we're beginning to envision an end to stocks of the necessary quantities of "renewable" resources from which paper is renewed. Paperlessness has entered the workplace as electronic communication becomes more commonplace. But fossil fuels continue to burn to turn the turbines, which produce the electricity to make electronic communicating possible. So there's not much being gained.

Just today, I watched with nostalgia and some envy as three eighth grade boys worked hard at playing with paper airplanes. Some of their products were amazing; others never made it off the test runway. One of the boys is severely emotionally disturbed, but has progressed remarkably over the last six years, so he can now compete and cooperate with others, have fun in a group, and participate appropriately in class. Another is labeled *learning disabled*, but he held interest while losing two games of chess yesterday. The third has cystic fibrosis, and his life dreams must be shorter than the others' – he may have lived half of his life already.

The term, *paper tiger*, is used to describe an entity that is long on rhetoric and short on action. The *paper tiger* takes much and gives little. If we are to help children and schools, we have to be long on paper books, paper reports and evaluations, paper for student use, and paper money to sustain the process of learning; and we must approach life with the strength and grace of a *real tiger*, which instinctively protects its young. And we must understand that to have left any child behind we must have been somewhere other than where the child was. As long as we *stay with them*, without giving up, accepting mistakes as learning and cutting some slack for those whose life prognoses are not good, we can't possibly leave any children behind.
Shabbat Shalom, Dad

~ EVERY FRIDAY: SHABBAT SHALOM FROM A GENTILE FATHER ~

May 14, 2004

Shabbat Shnoise

Here is a poem that came to me as I brought in the bird feeders for the night. Hope you like it.

NOISY NIGHT
It's a noisy night in Nature's neighborhood.
Just open any window or door
And hear tree frogs sing prayers of thanksgiving
For yesterday's rain.
In the distance - not too far -
An owl tunes up for its part in the symphony.
Fish splash in the lake,
And a sleepy Great Blue Heron
Croaks a protest for the disturbance.
Bugs and beetles add a little zing to the song.
The neighbors' dogs talk to each other
As Abby joins in the conversation.
Yet midst all this noisiness,
Deer and raccoons make their silent,
Stealthy way through the yard.
It's a noisy night,
And we are the richer for it,
And grateful.
Love, Dad

May 21, 2004

Shabbat Shtest

Dear Grown-up Kids,

The ACT results were back for the 11th graders yesterday, so I did some quick calcs and talked to the kids about interpreting their numbers. We had a range from 15 to 30 (compares to last year's 15 to 25 and the previous year's 11 to 33) with a mean of 21 – pretty "normal" looking distribution for a class of 17. Illinois and Colorado are experimenting with using the ACT as a diagnostic test, so each state, viz. every school district, administers the ACT to all 11th graders who show up to take it – in our case 100%.

Test Battery

Let's test everyone over everything.

Starting Monday the following work-week daily battery of tests is scheduled:

1. Wake-up America Test (WuAT): Those who fail the test will be sleep deprived until they are able to wake up and smell the coffee.
2. Test of Toileting (TOT): Anyone who fails this test will have to wear a diaper or Depends, dispensation depending on the dependence level.
3. Test of Tooth Brushing and Flossing (ToTBaF): Failing this test results in social exclusion and daily sessions with the Tooth Fairy.
4. Test of Dressing (TOD): The acronym, TOD, the German word for "dead," implies that those who do not "dress to kill" will be reassigned to government jobs in northwest Missouri or Yemen.
5. Test of Breakfasting (TOB): Failure to take adequate time for or to put adequate materials into a healthful breakfast will result in a forced diet of unsweetened cream of wheat.
6. Test of Going to Work (TOGTW): Failure to travel safely to work in a timely fashion will result in being put in charge of reconstruction of the Great San Diego Garage, AKA Interstate 5.
7. At Work Exam (AWE): Failure to pass the AWE will result in being fired by Donald Trump.
8. Break Time Exam (BTE): The BTE is prerequisite to taking the LTAT. It must be taken, and can never really be failed. There is no real reason for it, but then there was no real reason for taking a break in the first place.
9. Lunchtime Analogies Test (LTAT): Those who pass the BTE may take the LTAT. The LTAT is a timed test normed by sex. Women who finish this test late may find themselves too dysphoric to attend to proper nourishment of body, mind, and soul. Men who don't pay attention to the women taking this test just don't get it.
10. Home-Going Test (HoGT): Failure results in being bound forever 'neath the streets of Boston.
11. Dinner Test (DTs): Too many before dinner drinks are sure to result in failure of this test. Too much wine with dinner may also contribute to skewed results. Too many after dinner drinks leads to ultimate collapse and cold turkey for the next several meals.
12. Bed Time Exam (BeTE): Many people never get this far in the daily battery unless they have a bunny with a drum. Those who do often go too far too soon. Those who failed test 11 usually don't get anywhere. Some people cheat. Catholics and Mormons erroneously think they've cornered the market. Failure of and success on this test is related to Gross Domestic Product. Testiness at bedtime is really gross! Although this is a hard test, those taking the test should be reassured of test ease prior to administration.

I doubt if ACT and College Board are going to endorse this vision of a daily-dozen testing battery. Remember that the test of happiness is the feeling of completeness one has by oneself and with another or others. You are both completely wonderful, and your parents are wonderfully blessed with happiness just to be able to watch your adult lives unfold. Many mitzvoth; Shabbat Shalom.
Love, Dad

May 28, 2004

Life Blanket
The blanket fell like snow in calm air,
Filling first one place, then another, and,
Falling, whooshed the air away
'Til there was no more anywhere, and
Everyone gasped to get one last
Breath of sweetness
Before it came to rest and
Covered everything
But memories.
Love, Dad

June 4, 2004

Shabbat Shmemories
Summer seemed forever coming and forever going when I was in elementary school. Now the school year flashes by too quickly and summers are mere commas in the sentence of time. Public education has always offered the perks of holidays, snow days, and summer vacations. As a child on the Amity farm, summer meant three months of helping in the garden; helping with the chores and housework; roaming the woods, fields, and pastures; bicycling on sparsely traveled country roads; playing with Blackie, then Ring; catching feral cats; fishing; driving a tractor for hay crews; riding Babe; watching vintage British movies and domestic soap operas on B&W TV; and walking beans – most of the summer spent in the company of adults, machines, animals, or alone. Town kids were objects of envy. According to their accounts of what they did on summer vacation, they got together with other kids to ride bikes and play baseball, kick the picket (we used sticks, not cans), and Monopoly.

But we traveled more than most. We went to Iowa several times per summer, and we never missed the Iowa Championship Rodeo in Sidney in August. Some oppressively hot and humid summer nights made sleep impossible indoors, so we moved mattresses and comforters and sheets to the front lawn to sleep, adventurously, under the great lighted canopy of the visible universe on a sea of dewy lawn. I'm sure the cattle in the adjacent pasture were amused. Summer's end was welcomed as an exciting time to prepare for and begin another endless school year.

Hard to believe that so many summers and school years have gone by. The fleetingness of these present years carries a warning and a challenge to those still young enough to measure time in moments: Live the life you can or must, but live it well, enjoy the ride, and appreciate the company.

Here's a song that crept into my head on the way to Car Care; it's a bossa nova piece.

Point of View

It all depends on our point of view,
As you see me and I see you,
Whether we are singles or together.
When we both see eye to eye,
See the moments racing by,
How we hope for, yet, one more tomorrow.
"Now" is just a memory for another day.
Dreams are made and fade like melting snow.
No regrets; they're fruitless agonizing.
Life holds many places yet to know.
So watch life from the mountain tops,
Or from some orbit deep in space,
And start the time that never, ever stops.
When you see from way out there
What will cause your heart to care,
Climb down here and meet life face to face.
It all depends on our point of view;
I'm glad to share my world with you.
Life is grand as long as we're together.
Together; together . . .

Shabbat Shalom
Love, Dad
P.S. Hope your birthday was out of this world, Robbie.

~ EVERY FRIDAY: SHABBAT SHALOM FROM A GENTILE FATHER ~

June 14, 2004

Shavua Tov

I was toving along counting blessings galore,
When out of the phone came a terrible roar.
Picked up the receiver and dared, with my ear
Placed on the earpiece, to listen and hear.
A most horrible roar, again rent the peace,
And put back in my pant legs last summer's sharp crease.
Holding the phone apart from my head,
And checking occasionally: Might I be dead?
I listened again to the elephant-like trumpets
That blared from the phone and made crumbs of my crumpets.
Then back in the back of the back of my mind,
I thought of a light that I had to find.
I searched on my scalp, on my neck and my arm,
And thought this is the thing that will save me from harm.
I looked on my leg and on down to my toes,
For the light I was seeking, all places it goes.
I looked in my tummy, my rummy, and spleen,
And finally found it aglowing faint green.
The light blinked, "Hello and how-do-you-do?"
And I said in a flash, "That depends upon you,"
And invited the green-glowing warmth to my ear,
And I asked it politely the noise to make clear.
Then quick as a wink in a blink of an eye
The horrible noise was trumping, "Bye-bye."
So I thanked the green glow, as I watched it turn blue
From taking the noise and turning it to
A symphony known to only a few,
Who are lucky enough to know children like you,
Who know, too, the healing power of the light,
And summon it needful by day or by night,
To quell the bad feelings and make them take flight
To land in a desert out of earshot and sight.
And the light then ascended to heavens above,
Where it waits for the calls from those full of love,
Who need to feel peaceful, and strong, and serene,
From the warmest cool glow that they've ever seen,
To visit each nose and each elbow and knee
With remarkable healing, and fill them with glee.

May you enjoy the energy of the light tonight and always.
Love, Dad

P.S. This is probably the last message from this address until ca. August 9. Tomorrow is my last day of work until then. Happy summer!

To: Lamelle & Rob Ryman
From: Larry Rawlins
Date: August 9, 2004
Subject: **The Horse Crick House**

The last time I saw the Horse Crick house it was full of some farmer's hay.
No big dog leapt and yipped a welcome, nor did any rooster crow the morning to life.
The lots were gone and the sheds with them.
The gully was largely filled in, no longer a source of vertigo at its edge.
Many trees were gone in favor of corn growing green on still steep, now terraced hills.
Three children were born in rented houses, one would be born here and another in Hand.
All five would sense this place as Home –
This place that Dad built with native lumber
And Mom labored in as the Home Maker.
Dad was proud of the extra wide soffits, which all agreed made the house look larger.
How a family of seven* managed to live peaceably
In this square box of four rooms is amazing!
That we left that place, which was electrified,
And moved to a yet smaller bottomland rental shell,
Without the benefits of electricity,
Is even more unbelievable.
The Horse Crick House was the first home for all of the family*.
The house is gone now.
The memory of Dad's house, Mom's home, our first home,
Full of hay and in decay is sad.
Yet moving on was a right decision,
And each subsequent house was made Home
With the same love and skill at surviving.
There may be no family reunions
At the Horse Crick farm,
But it won't hurt to remember
That it was once the center of family life,
The family's first owned Home.

Happy homing in on your family's life center.
Love, Dad

*By the time I was born Irma was married and 5 months pregnant, living in California, having followed Mom's family west [at some point returning to Horse Crick when Frank was sent to Hawaii during WW2], and Kent was in the South Pacific fighting the war. So the five of us kids never really lived all together. It occurs to me that the folks did the same thing to Kent and me – sold out and moved while we were away in our respective wars. So neither of us came "home" to the place we left. Of course, Kent wasn't married and I was; but Melanie and I weren't exactly settled yet. I have no memories of living at Horse Crick, in southwest Iowa's Missouri River bluffs, but I remember visiting the people who bought the farm and Dad getting into the Horse Crick House attic to retrieve our electrical appliances when the REA came to the Payne house.

August 13, 2004

Pursuit of Sanctuary
Can you remember a time, a certain place,
When and where you felt enormous peace,
A sense of belonging,
Absolute, pure safety?
The pursuit of sanctuary,
Thus defined,
Is worthy as a goal
For every day and every life.
Just as sleep is the body's sanctuary
From physical and emotional stress,
The personal sanctuary,
Whether it is a place
Or a meditative state,
Is crucial to rejuvenation
Of the embattled self.
Since we cannot always
Choose our battles,
We should cherish choosing our sanctuaries.
Today, my sanctuaries include
Waking up next to Melanie (and Abby),
Writing to you,
Enjoying good coffee,
Anticipating our upcoming visit to West 96th Street,
And knowing that I have Home
To return to after work.
Amid the stress
Of moving and movers,
Of learning the ropes in a new city
And a new neighborhood,
Of becoming acclimated to a new apartment,
Of beginning a new job,
Of bearing the burden of the future,
However joyfully,
Remember to choose, also,
Sacred moments in sanctuary,
In pure safety and love.
Shabbat Shalom, Dad

August 20, 2004

Dear Kids,

I heard an interesting interview on Morning Edition on the way to work - female singer-songwriter, who I am sure must be famous. Anyway, it started a melody and poem fragment in my head. I've laid it down here to try to quiet it, so I can get more work done, and I hoped you might possibly like it. The scene is Man with Woman; self-talk inside one head or both; questioning the validity of something deeply desired; and almost missing the message because of all the internal noise.

Love in Question?
Whenever we find ourselves together,
Do we ever really find ourselves?
Or are the words just superficial -
Familiar, practiced banter that's gone on forever?

Tell me what is on your mind.
Tell me what new truths you find in the world around us,
In the space between us.
What will waken all our senses and eliminate defenses?

Tell me what is on your mind.
I can take it if you're kind.
What, now, are the issues, can't be wiped away with tissues?
What will make us stronger, make our life together longer?
Tell me what contract we signed that says love must be maligned.
The fire of youth may die out,
But inside I hear it cry out.
Yesterday: we can't reclaim it.
But tomorrow: we can tame it.
What will make us stronger,
Make our lives a little longer?
What will waken all our senses,
And eliminate defenses . . .

Whenever we find ourselves together,
Do we ever really find ourselves?
Or are the words just superficial -
Familiar, practiced banter that's gone on forever?
Take for granted what we're feeling;
What's this bargain that we're sealing?
What's this hand that you are dealing,
While my mind's forever reeling?
Did I hear you say you love me?

It may never make the charts, but at least it got to New York.
I love you. Shabbat Shalom, Dad

~ EVERY FRIDAY: SHABBAT SHALOM FROM A GENTILE FATHER ~

August 27, 2004

Relax

Before you become calm,
You will do a couple of other things.
One is a deep breath,
The other is another deep breath.
And just before, on the cusp of calm,
You may smile or chuckle or chortle.
Have you ever wondered
What would make a turtle chortle?
Me either, but now that I mention it,
I think a turtle would chortle
Hearing a woodchuck chuckle,
Which would chuckle
Watching a snail smile,
Which would smile
Watching you take a third deep breath,
Which might really be a sigh,
One can't be too sure about such things,
And who's counting anyway?
I am counting the minutes to be had
'Til we're together in your Manhattan pad.
And pay attention to your breathing,
As you soar on wings of pro-creativity,
Toward a lovely, loving destiny.
Shabbat Shalom,
Love, Dad

September 7, 2004

Loving Thoughts . . . Missing You

Hello New Yorkers,
Thanx for your warm, if damp, message and photos, Mom and I parted at the airport parking lot; Abby and I got home at about 11:30 pm, while she bunked at Leslie's house. Our faster-than-clockwork flying experience took a nosedive on the last leg; the American Eagle connection from Chicago to Moline was more than an hour late.

Thanks for hosting our party time in Manhattan. Surely we left less work to be done next time back east. Actually, I feel really good being useful to such resourceful kids. Of course, I expect both of you to take notes. Remember:

>Given a reasonable quantity of soap, water, and scrubbing
>Any amount of grime will wash off;
>A fly in the ointment doesn't necessarily contaminate the whole oint;
>There is more harmful bacteria in your mouth than any other part of your anatomy –
>In extreme cases it contributes to trash talk or diarrhea of the mouth;
>A good thought shared helps you and everyone around you,
>And a bad thought held in leads to perseveration and contributes to depression;
>Love and companionship are the most precious of human values;
>In the fat-cow years build more granaries;
>Avoid debt that isn't also an investment;
>Live well today and tomorrow will surprise you anyway;
>There is only one small *i* in both MARRiAGE and FAMiLY;
>You will enjoy life in proportion to the joy you bring to others;
>There comes a time when work comes first –
>This is my time.
>Take the best of care of the three of you.
>Love, Dad

~ EVERY FRIDAY: SHABBAT SHALOM FROM A GENTILE FATHER ~

September 17, 2004

Shabbat Shannah Tova
Whether years are numbered in the 5,000s or the 2,000s, the most important number is the one we use for *Now*. I wish some things from the past could be changed – throughout lots and lots of recorded history (and myth). Yet *Now* wouldn't be *Now* without that past and that record. Everything we perceive and do *Now* is filtered through what was. Also, everything we see as possible goes through the same sieve. Sometimes we need to suspend our past-based "reality" in order to accomplish something *Now*. *Now* that the air is cleared, the mind refreshed, the past forgiven and treasured, may you find yourselves at peace with the decisions that made *Now* happen for you, and may you enjoy each other in the next year of reality as only you can create. *Now* is always Number 1, and you are always *Now*.
Love, Dad

October 1, 2004

Shabbat Shuremissyou

I'd Rather Be with You
I'd rather be with you, just to know you're OK.
I'd rather be there or here or anywhere *with* you.
Instead, I'm here with the advent of Illinois' autumn,
Expecting not the welcome, startled bark of life,
But the startling north wind and first frost.
I'd rather be with you, just to hear your wisdom.
I'd rather be there or here or anywhere to *hear* you.
Instead, I'm here where the village siren just announced noon,
As if the sun would stop at apex should it be silent,
And history and future would be forever the same.
I'd rather be with you, so I could see you.
I'd rather be there or here or anywhere so I could watch.
Instead, I'm here with memories of tears and rain,
Of lost and found things, of searches and discoveries,
And the newness of fresh-washed-earth and sunshine.
I'd rather be with you, so I could lift your burdens.
I'd rather be there or here or anywhere; and that I could.
Instead, I'm here with the family's hope for your family,
And felt-certainty that, in the end, *Everything* will be all right.
I'd rather be with you.
And you know that when you need me,
I will be.
I Love You, Dad

October 22, 2004

Shabbat Shmoving

The famous systems-theory therapist, Virginia Satir, said, "When you're stuck, move."
Being stuck conjures memories like:
Tractors mired to the axel in the rich wetness of the creek bottom;
Cars hopelessly caught in vast snowdrifts;
A car going nowhere on a centuries-old accumulation of smooth river rock;
Traffic creeping along a 'freeway," when there were places to be and things to do;
Impossible decisions in need of possibility.
A tractor sometimes would have been dug out of its predicament –
First, the farmer would release the load it was hauling – plow, disc, harrow, planter –
Then, one spade-full at a time, he'd dig space for it to find purchase and move.
Often another tractor would pull its cousin using a log chain.
A driver stuck in a snowdrift sometimes can get moving by rocking (& rolling) the car,
Slowly going forward and backward rhythmically, until the tires roll into freedom;
As for getting stuck on river rock, several hands and shoulders can get a car moving.
Being stuck in traffic is annoying to catastrophic in our deadline-conscious world.
Active research has shown that it is probably best to stay in the lane you're in.

So, when you're stuck, and you need to move,
Let go of the *extra* load you carry –
Take it up again when you're on solid footing.
Dig yourself out one chunk at a time;
Ask for and accept help*;
Develop a strategy and make it work;
Don't switch lanes until you've made it out,
And, above all, remember that you, and you alone, are the driver.

Love, Dad
*Especially the strength-to-strength kind; consider two tractors

~ EVERY FRIDAY: SHABBAT SHALOM FROM A GENTILE FATHER ~

October 29, 2004

Shabbat Shvote

Dear Kidz, Little Pickle, Haya, and the cricket in the corner.

A lot of folks are saying that they'll be glad when it's over.
Seems that too many people are being hurt –
Lots of fanatical miscreants crossing borders to do harm;
Friends turning on friends, relative on relative, neighbor on neighbor,
In a frenzy of propagandizing and power mongering.
Violence by word or deed seems the norm,
Elections, with enormous hopes and implications,
Being held under dubious circumstances,
With very little being done, or, perhaps, possible
To turn the turbulent tide.
Yes, a lot of folks will be glad to see November 3, 2004.

What must we remember? Among other events,
Remember . . . the Alamo . . . the Maine . . . Pearl Harbor . . . the Holocaust . . . 9/11.
So much violence inciting international conflicts. So much more violence!
Seems that the more we remember, and misremember,
The more convinced we become
That we can cure the world's ills by brute force.
We are such brutes, we Americans.

Bruting right along,
I hope your Shabbat is Shalomy,
That your time together is precious and loving,
That you find renewal and reinforcement
In down-time, dog-time, friends, and food,
And that you welcome the love
That somehow finds you
When you need it,
Even when you don't ask for or expect it.
Love, Dad

November 5, 2004

Shabbat Shhello

Dear Kids,
The following is an entirely extemporaneous parodical response to your news that is bound to get our beloved Pickle to face the music. I think you'll catch on to the melody:

Breeched?
Hello Pickle,
Well hello Pickle.
'Twould be nice if you would turn yourself around.
You make Mom swell Pickle.
I can tell, Pickle,
You're still growing, we're all crowing our love just abounds.
I heard the doc blurted
That you are inverted.
What would make you do that in a space so tight?
So, spin ag'in, Pickle.
Don't be so fickle now, Pickle.
Pickles are supposed to come out right.
Love, Grandpa

November 12, 2004

Leavin' Incensed
Dear LRPH,
The village quaint is what it ain't when leaves are set ablaze;
The incense of a trillion leaves can cause my eyes to glaze.
But in a while I'll leave these piles of autumn's last goodbye
To travel where the trees, though bare, allowed their leaves to fly.
Love, Dad

~ EVERY FRIDAY: SHABBAT SHALOM FROM A GENTILE FATHER ~

November 19, 2004

Dear Kids,
This has been a long week – the only 5-day school week in November. It's almost time for homeroom, so I'll have to do this quickly.

Focus
It's just a point out there. It's merely a millisecond of latitude coordinated with longitude hovering just out of reach, but clearly in view. Life seems too long to see it when you're ten and nobody you talk about is in a war. Life even seems possibly long in a war, dodging shells and malaria. At sixty, half or more of it is obviously in the past, so the forward view is foreshortened, so that point is still out there. And it's not anything like unexpected; it has, of course, always been there. Before, there was always a horizon in the way – the gorgeous glare of sunrises and sunsets that kept the eyes from seeing beyond. Now the ages 68 and 83 have more meaning, as do 81, 80, and 75; as do 27, 28 and .5. I am thankful that so many, especially a certain violinist, helped me to celebrate my 60th. I am thankful for the sacrifice of that violinist's life-mate, protestething naught. Most of all I am thankful for that point. I hope to keep it out there, in focus, for a long time. And I hope that *our* time will find true focus as the years go on. Forever hold hands, the sunrise, and sunset in your hearts.
Love, Dad

November 24, 2004

Dear Kids, Li'l Pickle, and Haya,
Mom is picking me up after work today; then we're off to B.C. Sounds sort of like time travel doesn't it? Let me see what I can conjure up in a few minutes here.

Healing Tears
And yet we will the tears to flow,
Again the dam won't let them go.
The evening mist, the morning frost
Escapes the lonely womb of night
To love the liquid morning light,
But we still will the tears to flow,
Again the dam won't let them go.
And then they kissed at some great cost,
Because the time seemed very right,
Undaunted they by fear of might,
And yet we will the tears to flow,
Again the dam won't let them go.

What was before, forever lost,
And though forever was in sight,
And though they vowed to stand and fight,

They could not will the tears to flow,
The dam just wouldn't let them go.
They hadn't missed some target tossed,
Nor had they cut and run in fright,
And conversations, kept polite,
The tears were there but would not flow,
Some dam just wouldn't let them go.
Yesterday a chasm crossed,
Today there's neither wrong nor right.
When, frostily, we face the light,
The kiss of sun on frost will show
The icy dam must melt, must go,
As healing tears will ever flow.
Love, Dad

December 3, 2004
Dear Two +,
Miss you dearly. Mom was one lucky mom. The Blazer performed well under the stress it encountered and kept her safe. I love you. Please use a quiet voice to read the following lines.

Shhhhhhh.
Listen.
If you're quiet enough in a quiet enough place
You can hear your own heart beat,
Hear the blood coursing through your veins,
Hear your sacred breath flowing in and out.

Shhhhhhh.
Listen.
Hear the last leaf fall from the maple tree,
Hear the first snowflake alight on your shoulder,
Hear the rabbit emerging from its warren,
Hear your lover's eyes blinking.

Shhhhhhh.
Listen.
Listen to life around and within you.
Hear the roots digging in for winter,
Hear truth as it must be known,
And hear the love of ages preparing to emerge.
Shhhhhhh.

Love, Dad

~ EVERY FRIDAY: SHABBAT SHALOM FROM A GENTILE FATHER ~

To: Larry Rawlins   From: Lamelle & Rob Ryman   Date: December 3, 2004   Subject: **Re: Shabbat Shhhhhhh**
Thanks for this whimsical poem! :-)   Did you check your email at home yet?   i (we) love you   ldr

December 3, 2004

Hellowwwwwwwwww!

Howdy Y'all,
Reckon as how ah done read th' email t' the house. Had quite a nice phoneversation with you two, too. Mehbe the hatchin' young'n'll get a kick outa yore very rural roots in the guize of contrived dialect. It's mah belief that yore happiness, laughter, and music resonate within. How's the Pa holdin' up? Bustin' 'is buttons, ah bet! Had to move mah own buttons leftward a bit to avoid strain on the fabric - and nary a pound gained.
Lovissimo,
Dad

To: Larry Rawlins   From: Lamelle Ryman   Date: December 3, 2004   Subject: **Re: Hellowwwwwwwwww!**
Well, howdy thar, Pa...soon ta be Grandpappy!! We's all sendin' yew olive our luv'n. I reckon the hatchling 'ill be speakin' like 'is er 'er rural roots lickety split like. The Pa here is doin' mighty fine. Good thing you moved dem buttons so as they di'n't bus' yer shirt open.   We luv yew mightily.   Kisses to Mammy.   xxxooo   Yer Young Hen

> **To:** Larry Rawlins
> **From:** Rob Ryman
> **Date:** December 3, 2004
> **Subject: Re: Hellowwwwwwwwww!**
>
> I reckon we's awful good, but busy, and mos assuredly gonna be on sum kinna rollacoaster, if ya ever saw one of them thar newfangled machines. They have'm at places they call "amusement parks," but when I saddled up to see one, i'z most disappointed. It was neither amusin' nor a park. Mosly a big ugly mess a concrete, these twisty twirly metal doodads high'r than a silo, and a buncha cryin' chllin', some who'd dun throwed up on theyselves.
> I love you,
> Billy Bob
>
> P.S. All of that was to say that I'm bustin' out all over! Feeling so excited, a real sense of purpose and mission and wonder.

December 10, 2004

Shabbat Shanukkah

Dear Kidz,

Good to hear your voices on the line, over the air, in the answering machine yesterday. Congrats, Robbie, on the feedback of confidence in your work. Interesting, Haya's reaction to David (is that name right for the baby?).

Season of Miracles

December is the season of miracles –
Christmas and Chanukah lighting much of the world.
Yet the December miracle closest to my heart is
The birth of the baby, Melanie.
Even Jesus wasn't born on the ass Mary rode.
But Melanie was born in the back seat of a Chevy,
And the oil that burned bright for eight days of old
Neither illuminated nor warmed Jacquetta's birthing progress.
And the sand and stone of the road to Bethlehem
Bore no threat to safety as the ice on U.S. 71.
Or had the oil not prevailed,
Or had the Christmas story not been believed,
Or had the Chevy run off the road, as Chevies do,
The history of humankind would have gone askew,
And you, beautiful miracles, never would have been,
In this place or any other,
And the Miracle of Little Pickle
Would be a Story untold.
In Love and Awe of All of Us,
I remain, truly yours, Dad

~ EVERY FRIDAY: SHABBAT SHALOM FROM A GENTILE FATHER ~

December 17, 2004

Bears and Bushes

Dear Lamelle, Robbie, Little Pickle, and Haya,

The poet's eye, in a fine frenzy rolling, Doth glance from heaven to earth, from earth to heaven,
And as imagination bodies forth The forms of things unknown, The poet's pen
Turns them to shapes and gives to airy nothing A local habitation and a name.
Such tricks hath strong imagination, That, if it would but apprehend some joy,
It comprehends some bringer of that joy, Or in the night, imagining some fear,
How easily is a bush supposed a bear!
(W.S.: Midsummer Night's Dream)

Shabbat Shhhower

I imagined my daughter, in the shower
Covered in blood that wasn't blood,
And wished I might have been there
To analyze the awful goo
And declare it what it was.
The dreadful is ever more so
With the knowledge of possibility –
The soldier's sharp reflexes
Knowing that only happenstance
Separates survivors from victims,
The traveler's helplessness
When the plane encounters real turbulence.
Therefore, it's important to see our *Selves*,
To observe from some second or third position
Of our minds, and dissociate from fear,
So it's possible to move rationally
Toward some painless conclusion,
Then re-associate in the knowing moment.
And the fellow soldiers and travelers will be comforted,
Also providing comfort by their presence,
Ready with us to confront the bear,
Even though it might be but a bush.

May you enjoy your blood and all it does.
May you bathe in pristine living water.
May you find places above pain
And always return to groundedness.
May you recognize bears and bushes for what they are
And love for all that it is and grows to become.
Love, Dad

2005 ✡ 5765

January 7, 2005

Shabbat Shcold

O wad some Power the giftie gie us
To see oursels as ithers see us!
    RB: "To a Louse"

I always liked Robert Burns.
The challenge of the dialect played a part.
Burns did well as long as he was true to his roots,
But when he attempted to take on the airs of aristocracy,
He lost much of his following and income.
My mother liked to recite the quotation above –
In passable dialect.
I think it's natural for her era's farm folk and others in poverty
To relate to Burns and to be philosophical about having merely enough.
They lived in a community of hard-working poor,
Who didn't realize or admit the extent of their impoverishment,
As long as they had sustenance and their community.
That community is gone now.
Today's poor realize only too well
The gulf between their lives and the lives of the wealthy.
I never considered myself rich –
Middle class, maybe, but never rich –
Yet, one time with a class of elementary children
Who were studying geography,
I seized upon the teaching moment
And invoked my travel experience.
They asked me if I had been to this or that country,
And often I had, so it was fun to be able to say yes to
Italy, Germany, Israel, Vietnam, England, France, Mexico, etc.
Then one very little boy said,
"Wow! Are you rich?"
I thought a couple of silent moments before I answered,
"Yes, I guess I am."
Let us enjoy the richness of our lives,
Whatever form it may take,
And gladly share our wealth
With those who see us as we are,
Teaching us to "see oursels as ithers see us."
    Love, Dad

P.S. It was around Zero degrees F this a.m. Colder forecast for tomorrow. Days are lengthening, spring is coming. Be cool and stay warm.

January 14, 2005

Look to this day:
It's snow and blow outside –
A great day in, looking out.
2nah salad lunch tasty,
Kids get out at 2:05 –
Last day of the semester –
So teachers can record grades,
Can't take long.
All of my "grades" are in –
Guess they're also out.
Car in and out of the shop,
Ready to haul us into Charleston,
Won't be too much snow.
Thanx for the money tips.
With no plan to crash soon,
We'll play it by ear PRN.
Play the hand that you're dealt,
Don't bluff each other,
Share your cards,
And always
Recognize
What is really, really important.
Love, Dad (Arf!)

January 21, 2005

Night
Night is bright with moonlight,
Maybe that explains why otherwise normal adults
Would be up and at 'em at such an hour.
This moment of midnight madness
Is brought to you by . . .
The Moooooooooon!
Thank goodness it's not Robbie's version of Walmart parking lot infamy.

The Drip

Sat down to work and heard the faucet's drip;
Too tired to walk the steps to turn it tight,
Yet tried to wake my senses so I might,
But didn't want to take the chance to trip
And find myself supine upon the floor.
The drip grows e'er more noisy- get a grip
Before you find yourself gone out of sight,
And either turn it left or turn it right
To keep your mind from yet another flip
And send you, in some madness, out the door.
Yet louder, still, the droplets splatter on;
What's left of my right mind is mostly gone.
May be too late to salvage brainy thought,
Lest Pickle would appear as thought she ought.

Love Dad, AKA Grand-Dad-In-Waiting

January 28, 2005

Shabout Shoutin': Six and a Half Flags over MidAmerica

The coaster was rollering o'er hill and o'er dale,
With slow climbs to the top and, then, without fail,
A hesitant moment followed close by a shriek,
As car after car tumb'd over the peak.
And quick in the curves that wove in and out
Twixt ever more hill tops; hear everyone shout
In anxious expecting of the next awful drop,
"I wish," said one rider, "that the whole thing would stop!"
And then, as if ans'ring the prayer of this lout,
It quitted. It halted. It stopped without doubt.
And all became quiet, too quiet for me,
For the coaster was toaster, for so I could see.
And as we made exit to climb t'ward the ground
We looked at the tracks and the cars all around,
Including the Wisher, whose whimsical wish
Turned something of fun to a thing like a fish
Out of water too long, out of breath, so it lay,
Like a sculpture of steel, and unwilling to play.
And everyone climbing complained of this boor
For not doing the job that it was made for.
But the one who had wished, wished again in his head
That all could be coast'ring and shrieking instead.
For it's obvious, plain to see why it's there:

~ EVERY FRIDAY: SHABBAT SHALOM FROM A GENTILE FATHER ~

To quicken our spirits, to answer a dare,
To thrill to the Hills and the Dailes as they go,
And conquer our fear for a moment or so.
To wish it to stop was a terrible wrong,
For it should go on – go on for as long
As it needs to, to bring people joy,
Although it seems like a monstrous toy,
To get people up and to let the same down,
It's wrong to expect it the other way 'round.
We're so glad when it runs the way that it should,
And he wished in his heart that all of them could
Be climbing the hill near the end of the run,
Expecting the shrieking and feeling the fun.
And, flash! They were back there ashrieking with glee,
Then the cars slowed to a crawl and set them all free.
The lesson was learnt by that wisher in fright
That it's ever more fearful to have something in sight
And then lose its context, its role in life's schemes.
As the coaster was there for the fun of the screams.
Love, Dad
(Our first grandchild was born three days later.)

March 11, 2005

Shabbat Shdoors
Have you ever thought much of doors?
Doors come in many shapes, sizes, and weights.
Some doors are solid and opaque.
Is there a tiger on the other side?
Some doors have peep holes in them.
You can see most of what is on the other side,
But the view is distorted, and you have to be
Very close to the door to make your observation.

Other doors have some kind of window.
Some of the door windows are "frosted,"
Letting light in but with no good view of the other side
Even though you may see that something is there.
Some of the door windows are clear
Showing the outside to those inside
And the inside to those outside;
Privacy can be a problem.
Some doors are "Dutch" doors.
They have no glass windows
But the top half can open to the outside
While the bottom half can stay in place.

Dutch doors have the optimal window:
The view is not obstructed,
Small children and animals can't traverse them,
And air can flow freely in and out.

Other doors revolve.
They are in a constant state of opening and closing,
Allowing access and regress
Without ever exposing the interior to the elements.

Some cars have doors that move up and down.
Some doors have doors cut into them.
Doors can be wide and accepting or small and obstructive.
Doors can swing, slide, roll, or move on a track.
Doors can be fitted with locks,
Or they can be allowed to open easily.
Some doors are designed to keep in,
And others are meant to keep out.

Imagine the most beautiful house you'd ever want.
Imagine that someone gifted you this house.
Imagine that house without doors of any kind.
Wouldn't doors be the first modifications you'd make?
What kind of doors do you want for your house?
It's up to you.
Will your doors keep in more or keep out more?
Who will have keys to the locks?

Every door you go through on Shabbat
Is a door with my presence and love.
I will wait for you at each threshold.
There is no toll for passage.
Love, Dad

~ EVERY FRIDAY: SHABBAT SHALOM FROM A GENTILE FATHER ~

March 18, 2005

Hi Kidz,

I'm waiting for "Joseph" to start at 7:30. Theresa and I and maybe some others are going to have some dinner together somewhere.

If the World Was Upside Down
If the world was upside down,
If the arctic was *ant* and Antarctic *antless*,
If the Pacific was east and the Atlantic west,
If the Caribbean was frigid,
If the Empire State was in the deep South,
If the sun came up westward and went down in the east,
If the moon followed suit,
If the way to Grandmother's house was through the river and over the woods,
If Earth was 6th in orbit around the sun,
If the best movies came to Macomb first,
If Broadway actors longed to work off Broadway and in summer stock;
If the world was upside down
It would make little difference to me
As long as we know the real social security that is family,
As long as our love and caring for each other remains upright,
As long as we can hold our heads high for having taken the high road,
And as long as we hold each other's hands on the journey.
Love, Dad/Grandpa

April 1, 2005

Hope School

In temp'rate climes the seasons change again,
And winter's bleakness passes into spring's
Abundant blossoms, leafing trees, and things
To do in short sleeves and renewing rain.

The grass of green and flowers of gold retain
Their parents' hues and shapes; their fragrance brings
Familiarity and thoughts of swings
And slipp'ry slides, and recess on the plain,

Where ev'ry child could roam and learn of life
From sources pure and free of human taint;
As ev'ry day must have its wonder dawn,
When ev'ry person learns to handle strife
While leaning on the closest standing saint.

The hope of spring is in us each new day,
When we accept the blessings of child's play.

Shabbat Shalom, Dad
P.S. Tomorrow is the 109th anniversary of my father's birth.

~ EVERY FRIDAY: SHABBAT SHALOM FROM A GENTILE FATHER ~

April 7, 2005

Shabbat Shthursday

Hi Kids,
I have an appointment to talk with a 3rd grade boy, then I'm going to leave sometime before 2:30 p.m. Hope Rob can get some rest upon his return from company outing. We will expect an evaluation of the effort he and the company made.

I sent a couple of poems to the Illinois Association for Adult Development and Aging (IAADA) Newsletter editor last night. I was going to write something new, but time and tide intervened, so I sent November pieces – one from 1992, the other from 2002. I must wax poetic of age around the time of my birthday.

Let's see what Progoff provides this lunch moment.

Rain
Forecast
Not too much
'Twill soak in fast
Nurturing
Blossoms
Fresh

May your weekend and reunion be renewing as rain, and colorful and sweet as blossoms in spring.
Love and Shalom, Dad

April 15, 2005

Shabbat Shcontest

It's music contest day at Avon, and I'm judging choral sight-reading. It's been fairly easy on the ears but reminds me of why I looked elsewhere within education for a professional identity. Attend to the lines, the dynamics, the textures, the contrasts and repetitions of music as life, itself. No one can take from you the joy experienced in the presence of beautifully crafted music beautifully performed. Live each day in harmony with those around you. Enjoy the steps and leaps throughout life the best you can. Get into a rhythm and stay there as long as it's good for you. Make the cadences lovely and segues logical. If you must be angry, look to the root of it to learn its progression in your life, then find a restful resolution. Be kind to your fellow performers, for they are doing the best that they can, as you are. Kindness given is kindness received. Let each voice be heard and watch the director.
Love, Dad

April 29, 2005

Shabbat Shwanderings

Hi Y'all,
I have two must-dos today – prepare test materials for shipping and prepare the 8th graders for "Welcome to the Real World" (an event scheduled for 5/5/05). Naturally, I have to sub in math two periods today, so it will stretch me to get the other things done. Oh, well.

Progaffianly:
With the high price of gasoline, think of all the money we save whenever we pass gas . . .

stations. We could take those savings and invest them in privatized accounts, and live comfortably in retirement for some time to come, provided that much time comes.

Ironically, poor people and New Yorkers would save the most, because they don't drive much, and they eat a lot of beans and chickpeas. Now is the time to look ahead and nail down those retirement chateaus. I saw a listing in East Hampton that looked terrific for only $15,500,000. With inflation (or stagflation) rearing up, it would be best to snatch it up now before it goes up another half mil (a mere 3.2%) tomorrow. Why, with that savings, you could also buy the 3100 square foot cottage on Kiawah Island, SC. The possibilities are endless. Might as well pick up the Sears Tower, too. Wouldn't want to drop something like that! And the beauty of it al is that homeless children should be able to negotiate a bank loan for the deal, because the federal government will not leave them behind, and their SS benefits will be sufficiently recovered to cover any shortfall.

Four score and seven years ago was 1918. Our nation was only 53 years past the Civil War and just getting into the War to End All Wars – yeah, right! Four score and seven years from now your parents will be well into their hundreds and Neshama will wonder how she ever turned out to be so much like her mother after all; and her great grand children will be amazed at how early in her development she was able to roll from front to back.

So, should we bury Caesar or praise him? Probably, we should impeach him first – not Roman style, of course – *et tu Brute* – but with C-Span cameras and proverbial heads rolling. High crimes and misdemeanors. If anyone has ever missed his/her demeanor, it would be our current Caesar. *Et tu Dick*.

Let the good times roll! Of course the Dow has been rocking lately, back and forth, back and forth, Bach and . . . It's all rock and roll.

Thank you for being beautiful and smart, and capable and wise. Enjoy the wisdom of rest and rest your wisdom. Avoid blame and promote validations. Be good to and for each other.
Love, Dad

~ EVERY FRIDAY: SHABBAT SHALOM FROM A GENTILE FATHER ~

June 3, 2005

Glimpse of Next
Neshama crawling toward us,
Haya nervously settling in on the couch,
Lamelle's heartfelt "I love you" at the end of the mpeg.
Powerful seconds preserved on our computers.

The world has never looked better,
Never lovelier, never brighter or fair
Than now with the light of new discoveries.

The baby crawls to her future,
Parents eagerly making plans for the trip,
The way more clear in spite of any fog in the distance,
Crawling, standing, walking: no sedentary life style!

Blessings to you, who bless others with your lives.
Eagerly awaiting your safe, speedy arrival in Illinois.
Love and Meter, Dad/Grandpa

June 9, 2005

Shabbat Shorty Early

Dearest Four,
The electrician working on . . .I guess, electricity . . . has informed me that we will have none of that after 7:30 a.m. tomorrow. Hence, this early prose, or poetry, or . . . I guess, abuncha words. . . are being forwarded easterly as I steam and stew in my office, new, with some things taken out, some things thrown out, and some things shelved and drawered.

Lamelle, your addressing me as "Shorty" took me several places in the instant before I registered to what you alluded. Two related men of my previous generation were nicknamed, Shorty. One was your grandfather, J.E. Rawlins, who also answered to Ed or Edmond, but never to John, his first name. The other was "Aunt" Edith's husband, "Uncle" Seymour Stiles, whom we kids called Uncle Seym ("seem"), but whose wife usually called Shorty. Uncle Seym was shortier than Dad and plump (a good walking version of Humpty Dumpty), and neither man protested the *nom de mari*, as long as they were sleeping with the one speaking it. Size doesn't matter in most things, basketball, football, mini-submarine comfort not withstanding. I didn't know Uncle Seym very well. They lived in Colorado and were only occasional visitors in the Midwest as we were less frequent visitors in the Rocky Mt. foothills. Dad always thought they "put on airs" and considered themselves better than the average relative, just because they really did have more money than most. Kent and Layton spent some time with them and knew them much better than I. Speaking of size, "Aunt" Edith, Mom's first cousin, with whom Mom and her brother, Elbert, were raised, was the largest person in our family, in girth. I never knew her not to be extraordinarily heavy – even more so than Mom, who at 5 ft. 3 in. tipped the scales around 200 lbs.

Speaking of scales, not the type, which will never fall from politicians' eyes, but the kind one stands on to determine the mass of one's body in relation to gravity, mine checked in at a cool 165 the other day after racquetball. I want to be able to see those numbers at the end of sedentary day after I have had 3 squares and a chocolate malt. This has been a semi-sedentary day – Mom and I rode bikes 8.4 miles this morning and I played 9 holes of scrambled golf before arriving at work at noon. Work has been mostly unboxing and boxing stuff and making some room for my stuff. The A.D., whose former office this is, can't seym to get motivated to mine his own gold from this vein, so I'm just setting stuff outside in boxes. He does have a bad back and a bad heart, but I sorta resent straining mine on his behalf in this *forno*.

Tomorrow, being an unelectrified day in this building, I expect to leave at the end of registration, at noon. I may mow the lawn, which has grown in a few places to spite the drought. Or I may do whatever else Mom has suggested on those clever honey-do sheets mounted on the fridge.

Enjoy your evening, your work and Shabbat prep tomorrow, and most of all, enjoy each other. Keep the camera ready to mpeg that creepy, crawly baby. Still photography may never be sufficient from that first crawl onward. Laugh much, especially at yourselves, and always together. See your reflections in each other and marvel at them in the way Neshama did with the mirror – prime pix. Remember how precious each moment is, and let each one be full of joy and wonder.

Shabbat Shalom
Love, Shorty III

September 9, 2005

Hi kids. It wasn't a hurricane, but we had a thunderstorm yesterday evening that returned to us 1" of needed water. Hopefully, the p-boat is once again floating.

Post-Hurricane Ramblings and Rumblings

We were only just together, weren't we? Just a few days since, and we still feel lucky to have had those loving moments in a world where luck and love seem endangered. I guess there is no necessity to feel guilt when we compare ourselves to gulf coast [former] residents or Darfurians in peril, although somehow there is a tempering of soul to consider this richness that is ours against those kinds of backdrops. Human survival is a spiteful undertaking – *homo sapiens* exists in spite of its weaknesses as much as because of its strengths. We have yet to realize that we make up a global community, that we are affected by the trials and triumphs of others in the grand community, or that what we do or don't do affects everyone else – dominoes. As a species we are cocoonish and clannish, protectors of turf and defenders of independence. If our clan is strong and our cocoon is impenetrable, we flourish. If our turf bears abundant food and water we can maintain our strength and defend ourselves. Yet who is entitled to life in this strong, safe cocoon and clan? We were only just lucky, weren't we? And somehow most of us believe that the unlucky also deserve a chance at cocoonism. Maybe we can devote a portion of our strength toward strengthening other clans instead of destroying them. Then, we might find that the threads of our own cocoon become stronger and the life within better. And the world community – not a "new world order" – will become a part of each of us and we of others.

Stay safe and strong for each other. Love, Dad

October 3, 2005

Buon giorno e salve. So glad you are home safe and sound. Will want to hear about the journey in some detail.

Farming

I've had a busy day at the farm.
A bull calf was acting up in the lot,
So I cut him out of the herd
And brought him to my corral.
Some said he'd gotten into loco weed,
Others thought he had some other need.
At any rate, when returned to the herd,
He did a pretty good job of grazing.
So I gave him an extra helping of oats.
Calves are a lot like children.
They like to play,
Stay close to Mom,
And butt heads with other calves.
But, in the end, everything they do
Gives direction to what they become.
There are things that calves have no control over,
Like farmers and ranchers.
They trust dogs as a matter of choice, not necessity,
Because their kicks and butts can be lethal,
And smart dogs realize that fact.
A pack of dogs or coyotes can bring down a calf only if it is weak
And away from its mama.
So, I try to keep the herd together
Here on the farm –
Where the strong look after the weak,
And the weak seek strength in play,
And test the boundaries at times –
That's when I get called to bring 'em home.

Love, Dad

October 7, 2005

Shabbat Shalomest
Thanx for NER VID. Precious-*issimo*!
I got an email from Red Cross yesterday, so I may go to Gulf Coast next week. Should know by Monday or Tuesday. I would have to stay 2 weeks. Ron is nearly done with his part in the reconstruction from our own vile flood. Got results from recent blood test – all systems are go with proper numbers of reds and whites. Hope you are well and rested from your travels.

Back on the Farm
Calf calls for its mother,
But she is upwind and away and can't hear.
Calf gets a little crazy
Feels worried, trapped
Starts running,
Wrong direction
Away from herd
Wrangler goes after the maverick
And gives it just enough mothering
To keep it with the herd
Of course, the mother finds it
Because she depends on it for her comfort, too
Maverick's not very smart
Will have to relearn this lesson several times
Before really believing that being with
Is better than being apart
And safer, too, because of all the bogey dogies.
Be with, and enjoy.
Love, Dad

November 4, 2005

Shabbat Shpearls
Channel 51:
That's CNN here in my office.
And there you were, our beautiful girls,
Articulate mother, energetic daughter,
Involved friends,
Offering wisdom and happiness
That became, as it played out,
An ineluctable feeding of
Pearls to swine.
All of you and the viewers deserved better.
Have a peaceful Shabbat and find some new joy about each other to cherish.
Love, Dad/Grandpa

~ EVERY FRIDAY: SHABBAT SHALOM FROM A GENTILE FATHER ~

November 18, 2005

Shabbat Shmexico
The following was written originally in Spanish, with credit due to Google Translation.

Dear Children and Granddaughter,
I want to attempt this letter in Spanish, merely to discover if it is possible, with such limited knowledge of the language, to compose in the correct order a few cogent words. Additionally, I hope to become more familiar with the linguistic rhythm in advance of our upcoming meeting in Mexico. We are hoping for good health for everyone as we prepare for and embark on our holiday adventure. Shabbat Shalom, Beautiful Family. Get plenty of sleep, take good nourishment, be well, and be there when we are.
Your loving father/grandfather.

December 2, 2005

Hello, NYers!
"Well" is what Mom is not today – bronchitis. She saw the NP at 11:00 a.m. She got acoupla kinds of meds and went home to rest. How novel, and needed! How is Neshama? And Everyone? I have been totally tired at work since our spa adventure. Beginning to pull out of that mild malaise now. Noting your forecast for lots of snow, these reflections and deflections follow:

Snow Sonnet
Snow would not be so bad if it was warm.
A cruel twist of physics makes it cold
And causes folks to shiver, young and old,
Potentially to cause for them great harm.
Imagine, if you will, a pleasant storm
Of warm unmelting snowflakes one could fold
Or scoop into ice cream cones to be sold
With hot ice-sculptured sweets of varied form.
And all who walk the paths of Central Park
Or Boston Commons or Pacific strand
Could find a warm refreshment made of snow.
And for a dollar-fifty, on a lark,
Instead of Starbucks coffee cup in hand,
Warm snow would give the power to go.
But snow is what it is, of course that's true;
Let's hope the flakes that fall are blessings, too.
Love, Dad/Grandpa

December 16, 2005

O death, where is thy sting?
1st Corinthians, KJB

No Sting

Death doesn't scare me – not today, anyway.
The end of life has no particular lure, either.
Once there was a fascination with "crossing to the other side."
But some time ago those notions of eternal ecstasy died.
So here I am, unscared to death,
With a twinge of terror for the life that is left.
Knowing of some others' lives' woeful "winters,"
How easily I imagine myself ranting lunatic abuses,
Assaulting my neighbors, relatives, and friends with vulgarities.
That scene is set so easily, because only with practiced self control
Have I maintained the dignity to bury the old Midwest farmer in me.
Already, in the waning months of my fifth decade the self control is eclipsed,
And things that bother me become the object of vile objection. Privately now;
But certain to emerge from some closet at some inopportune moment,
When someone I love will realize that I – the practiced, public *I* – am really dead.
To be remembered, thus, in forethought is anathema.
Yet, once one is memory, anathemas may as well be laurels.
Rather than fearing the fetters of death,
I fear the awful freedom of senility.
Love, Dad

2006 ✡ 5766

~2006~

To: Lamelle & Rob Ryman
From: Larry Rawlins
Date: January 6, 2006
Subject: **Shabbat Shchool**

This . . .
Wilderness of untamed souls,
Laboratory of human hypotheses,
Cache of Future-fuel,
Tank of fluid trust,
Vial of virulence,
Tower of need,
Forest of flowering youth,
Prison of minds,
Definition of essential,
Echo of years before,
River of rapids descending,
Valley of meandering thought,
Pen of purposeful memory,
Mountain of misinformation,
Clock of ever-more-rapid ticking,
Life.
This place,
This one last leap of hope,
This **school**.
May you enjoy learning all your lives in the school of light and love.
Love Dad/Grandpa

January 13, 2006

Shabbat Shtest

Hi,
I haven't been avoiding you. I tried to call a couple of times. One time my phone charge went to zero. It's been an interesting day. I had very little traffic this morning, but the afternoon has been jammed, because the PLAN tests came back and all of the sophomores were in for interp. Just have two absentee students to do next week.

Test of Time

To stand the test of time requires possessing something utterly timeless, otherwise the thing or the idea would be tossed out into the chaos of nevermore, like yesterday's tea or last Sunday's Times. The computer age makes it easier to delete the unwanted, yet it seems that the more that's deleted the more is received to delete. With luck there will be something timeless in each of us that will keep us from oblivion. Then why is timelessness so fickle? Abraham Lincoln and Jack the Ripper have survived almost equally well in cultural memory, yet where one is worthy the other is an abomination. Oral history was a better preserver of timelessness of people than computers will ever be, but when whole cultures disappear or assimilate, or when we stop telling our stories and commit them to kindling, pages that burn for a while in our hearts and minds then in the bonfires of historical reconstructionism, the story stops, as if it never was. Let us, therefore, tell stories – truths and half-truths of existence that remind us more of our connectedness with history as we strive for a better future. Let us put words and pictures into the minds of children that will create timelessness, as they pass their updated version of those words and pictures to yet a next generation, like a gigantic, living umbilical passing through all generations from beginning to . . . timelessness.

Love (see you next weekend),
Dad/Grandpa

January 20, 2006

Briefly misplaced note:

Just before Lamelle and Neshama left for Illinois. (Withheld to preserve the surprise)

So. . .
As we who are apart are coming together,
Be it resolved to let the good times roll
And also to rock.
Good health, good fortune, and good mental status
Be ours for ever and ever,
Amen.
And should Elvis actually appeareat at the party
We would find that ever so jolly.
In the main,
Travel wisely, safely, and with energy.
Sustain each other in your various plights
And walk on the sunny side of the street.
After we rise on the third day hence,
We shall walk with you on the morrow.
Love, Dad/GP

January 27, 2006

Shabbat ShHappy Birthday

Dear Darling Granddaughter,
We'll celebrate together later, but for the first anniversary of your birth on Tuesday, I wanted to send you a special greeting. Let's see if something can roll off the fingers, onto the computer, and into cyberspace to your home.

To a Colorful Life
Life is like the spectrum of color,
And this is your special era for red.
The longest ray is all you'll know
Of distant years as your future grows.
Red is many things in various shades –
Apples, pomegranates (which, I think, means rock apple in French),
Strawberries, some raspberries, wagons, tricycles, lips, tongues, blood,
Ferraris, even Republican states at election time, of red are made.
Take sweet time through red years' hue,
They quickly fade to orange and yellow, then green and blue,
Like earth's grass and heaven's sky,
Pass by so fast they seem to fly.
Before you enter indigo,
Before experiencing vertigo,
Learn what you can from the longest ray.
Start with crimson each new day,
And dream of scarlet as you rest;
Life's longest view is always best.

Love and **Happy Birthday!**
Grandpa, loving you in Indigo

February 10, 2006

This month our juniors will take the Armed Services Vocational Aptitude Battery (ASVAB). This has set me to thinking about things military.

Military Bandsman's Parade

Go ahead and rain on my parade.
Let the generals get soaked as we pass in review.
We'll put soap bubbles in the trumpets
To produce an unforgettable effect
During "Ruffles and Flourishes."
And, maybe, instead of "Hail to the Chief,"
We'll play "God Save the King."
The latter speaks truer than the former.
Let the rain fall on those who reign.
Let *their* children and grandchildren lead
Their "Holy War" for capitalism
From the thick of the battle,
From the same ill-armored vehicles
On the same dangerous roadways
As those masses who really pay their dues.
We need this rain to end the drought of good sense,
To wash away the grime of crime in high places,
To make streams of navigable thought
That flow to tranquil seas of understanding.
Don't cancel the parade because of the rain.
Let the pomp and circumstance begin,
And remember that the uniform of the day
Does not include umbrellas.

May Shabbat cleanse you and keep you from the slings and arrows of outrageous politics.
May you be ever aware of how important others are in your lives and you in theirs.
May your Shabbat provide tranquility and protection from life's storms.
May you feel loved and love in turn.
May you grow beyond your physical development toward being at peace with yourselves as you implant peace in the world around you.
Love, Dad/Grandpa

February 13, 2006

Hi New Yorskimos! I've read in the Times of your blizzard and seen your pix. Thought I'd share one of my blizzards.

Mazzura Blizzard of 195X

I remember snow that was Snow,
Like you've just had, though
Not as much, ever, never
Much more than a foot,
With howling wind so clever
That it found ways to blow
Down the chimney and dampen soot,
And douse the cook stove flame,
And send tendrils of snow
Right 'round a closed pane.
Then, waking between blankets,
Under two thick comforters in a freezing room;
Sunlight, magnified by a white world of wonder,
Blazing bright and calm – true peace.
After breakfast, outside to play in the icy fleece,
To walk across the tops of fences,
Tunneling through drifts, exciting senses,
Making forts, falling, diving, listening
To the muffled winter of glistening
Splendor, and carefree hours between chores,
Never longing for tropical shores
That would never know this scene,
This dazzling departure from summer's green.
And then, at last, my mother calls, "Let's eat!"
The special feeling of fresh, dry clothes,
And noon-time dinner – potatoes, green beans, and meat,
A plate of bread at table's mid,
Milk, fresh just the night before,
And after a simple prayer was bid,
While wet clothes dried upon the floor,
We'd have our fill of a meal, gourmet,
Getting ready to explore yet more,
Of the arctic world in wintery play.
Love, Dad/Grandpa

February 24, 2006

Shabbat Shinterviews

Dear Loved Ones,
Being interviewed for jobs and schools is nice.
It means that someone really wants to talk with you,
To know you better, to see which shaped peg you are, if you fit.
That's kind of scary from my perspective.
What if someone interviewed me, and they thought I'd fit?
I can fit any given mold for only a few weeks, tops.
What will happen to me when they discover that??
One day at my current unfitting job
The superintendent kicked me out of a School Improvement Plan meeting.
Now, I'm all for school improvement, and I expect to participate in discussions –
Oh, I get it. That's the problem: There wasn't supposed to be real dialogue.
I have a glottal reflex against swallowing just any old idea
That happens to be in contemporary vogue.
So it was inevitable. Nobody in power wants discussion.
It's not that I have all the answers, but often there are a few unanswered questions.
At the risk of sounding cynical, and not a little vain,
May I remind the world that "blind faith is no faith?"
Keep your spirits (not the liquid kind) up as you embark on the next leg of the journey.
Get what you want and want what you get.
It's exciting to be related to you.
Looking forward to the next report –
I remain, blessed and with blessings,
Your proud Dad/Grandpa

March 3, 2006

Box Canyons
Without close neighbors and playmates near our farm, much of my childhood was spent pretending. Mostly I pretended that I was a do-gooder cowboy in the image of Roy Rogers, Gene Autry, Hopalong Cassidy, or The Lone Ranger. Movies in Maysville cost a dime on Saturday morning and popcorn was a nickel – the best 15 cents my parents ever spent. It seemed that the bad guys were always ambushing good guys or getting trapped, themselves, in some box canyon. We northwest Missourians had more hills than the western Illinois prairie, but not a single canyon – box or otherwise.

Learning to stay out of traps is a useful lesson for kids. Now we tell adults who are inexorably trapped in a "box" to think outside of it. Many types of boxes come to mind – jobs that don't fit, college majors that are no longer interesting, dysfunctional relationships and environments, government rules and regulations, "blind faith" toward just about anything – to name a few. The key to avoiding boxed entrapment is to guard your flank and leave a way out. Every good cowboy knows that.

Students entering college, the military, or the civilian workforce need to think like good cowboys and cowgirls. Young people tend to see the end of the world at the ends of their noses. When confronted with a problem, it looms so near and large that youngsters often fail to see the way out that was there all along. There is a job out there in the world that fits. There is no college major that can't be changed. There are redeeming social relationships and environments within reach. Government rules and regulations can be changed. Blind faith can become informed faith. And, except in trauma and life-threatening circumstances, problems are further from your nose and are smaller than first you thought. There is no better time to realize these ideas than when you are young and have the time and resiliency to recover from mistakes and miscalculations. The only real mistake one can make is to fail to learn from the experience and change directions – out of the box. Hi yo Silver, away!

Love, Dad

March 17, 2006
Shabbat ShVA

Dear Kids,
I'm going to the VA hospital in Iowa City soon to get some different hearing aids. Now that the VA has recognized that the Chinook noise in Vietnam was the major cause of my hearing loss, I have been given a 10% disability in my right ear (guess my left ear wasn't along for the ride). Anyway. That's enough to qualify for VA hearing aids. I'll let you know how it goes.
Love, Dad

To: Larry Rawlins From: Lamelle & Rob Ryman Date: March 17, 2006 Subject: **Re: Shabbat ShVA**
FYI Pard: New Hearing Aid Technology Coming Soon to a Theater Near You (or VA Hospital) Check out this website [about *Lyric* technology]-- I love you. RR

To: Lamelle & Rob Ryman From: Larry Rawlins Date: March 17, 2006 Subject: **Shabbat Shearing**
Thanx, Son Robert, Maybe there will be a *Lyric* in my ear-ic some near year-ic. Love, Dad

To: Larry Rawlins From: Lamelle & Rob Ryman Date: March 17, 2006 Subject: **Re: Shabbat ShVA**
Very cutie!! love you ldr

To: Larry Rawlins From: Lamelle & Rob Ryman Date: March 17, 2006 Subject: **Re: Shabbat ShVA**
Thanks for the chuckle Love Son Robert

March 24, 2006

Hi kids. About time to go home and to meet with the mayor again. Hopefulness is not *ness*isarily abundant.

The Fortunate Adventures of Ness

Ness was watching a spider climb to the top of the drain spout, and it started to rain. The spider spun a yellow slicker, a rain hat, and an umbrella and continued climbing with its otherwise unoccupied legs.

Ness was listening to a shepherd boy crying, "Wolf! Wolf!" When the adults got there with their weapons, they saw there was no wolf, but one of them stayed with the boy and the sheep, just in case. When the wolf did arrive, the man and the boy threw rocks at it and it left the sheep alone.

Ness was listening to a conversation between a nurse and an English patient. The patient was in great pain, took the prescribed medication PRN, and felt all the better by reminiscing about his love of living in the desert.

Ness watched a fight between two strong boxers and marveled at the way that each seemed to be able to parry the blows of the other until the very last round, when one boxer started to make progress and emerged victorious.

Ness was listening to a story about a monster in a Scottish lake, hanging on every word – Happi, Shy, One, Resourceful, Sad, Hopeful, Tough, Rich, Thankful, Truthful, Worthi, and many others, especially **Well.**

Well, *Ness* be yours entirely this Shabbat. Enjoy the certainty of triumph over Ill, *Ness*.
Shabbat Shalom, Dad

April 11, 2006

Good Pesach
When all the questions are asked
And all the answers are received
And the bitter memories of millennia
Are give to taste,
May you know peace in your house
Even as the Children knew peace
From the plague,
Even as we would know sweet peace
In our lifetime,
So we can all look forward
Without fear to
Next Year in Jerusalem.
Love, Dad

To: Lamelle & Rob Ryman
From: Larry Rawlins
Date: January 3, 2008
Subject: **One Year Ago**

Everybody remember what we were all doing one year ago today?

The sterile halls, the crowded waiting rooms, the anxious hearts that beat together, that ached together for the sake of the precious child we all love. Let us continue to ache, and beat, and wait, and love.

Love, Dad

~Afterword~

I hope you have enjoyed these love-letters-to-family and that you might recommend the book to others. The goal of writing these pieces was to communicate with my Jewish daughter and her modern orthodox family in a timely way – to give them blessings across our miles of separation. Since writing these pieces a lot of life has happened. The baby, Neshama, born in 2005 now has two delightful siblings: a sister, Aliya, and a brother, Shalev. The family still resides in New York City, so the maternal grandparents have learned the way there from western Illinois. Since our retirement we Midwesterners and the New Yorkers try to get together four or more times each year.

There have been more than the usual childhood maladies to contend with, and that story continues. The family is fortunate to be connected with a wonderful, supportive synagogue.

Larry Rawlins, M.M., Ph.D., L.C.P.C.

Made in the USA
Middletown, DE
07 August 2018